GOD'S CONSTANT PRESENCE

True Stories of Everyday Miracles

Strengthened *by* His Touch

EDITORS OF GUIDEPOSTS

with James Stuart Bell

 Guideposts

Strengthened by His Touch

Published by Guideposts
100 Reserve Road, Suite E200
Danbury, CT 06810
Guideposts.org

Acknowledgments

Every attempt has been made to credit the sources of copyrighted material used in this book. If any such acknowledgment has been inadvertently omitted or miscredited, receipt of such information would be appreciated.

Scripture quotations marked (AMP) are taken from the *Amplified Bible*. Copyright © 2015 by The Lockman Foundation, La Habra, California. All rights reserved.

Scripture quotations marked (ESV) are taken from the *Holy Bible, English Standard Version*. Copyright © 2001 by Crossway Bibles, a division of Good News Publishers. Used by permission. All rights reserved.

Scripture quotations marked (ISV) are taken from the *Holy Bible, International Standard Version*. Copyright © 1995-2014 by ISV Foundation. All rights reserved internationally. Used by permission of Davidson Press, LLC.

Scripture quotations marked (KJV) are taken from the *King James Version of the Bible*.

Scripture quotations marked (MSG) are taken from *The Message*. Copyright © 1993, 1994, 1995, 1996, 2000, 2001, 2002 by Eugene H. Peterson.

Scripture quotations marked (NASB) are taken from the *New American Standard Bible®*, Copyright © 1960, 1971, 1977, 1995, 2020 by The Lockman Foundation. All rights reserved.

Scripture quotations marked (NIV) are taken from *The Holy Bible, New International Version*. Copyright © 1973, 1978, 1984, 2011 by Biblica, Inc. Used by permission of Zondervan. All rights reserved worldwide. zondervan.com

Scripture quotations marked (NKJV) are taken from *The Holy Bible, New King James Version*. Copyright © 1982 by Thomas Nelson.

Scripture quotations marked (NLT) are taken from the *Holy Bible, New Living Translation*. Copyright © 1996, 2004, 2007 by Tyndale House Foundation. Used by permission of Tyndale House Publishers Inc., Carol Stream, Illinois. All rights reserved.

Cover and interior design by Serena Fox Design Company
Cover photo by Dreamstime
Typeset by Aptara, Inc.

ISBN 978-1-961126-36-7 (hardcover)
ISBN 978-1-957935-95-9 (epub)

Printed and bound in the United States of America
10 9 8 7 6 5 4 3 2

All of us want the assurance of not being deserted *by* life nor deserted *in* life. Faith teaches us that God is—that He is the fact of life from which all other things take their meaning and reality.

—Howard Thurman, theologian

TABLE *of* CONTENTS

Never Alone

By Bob Hostetler

I FONDLY REMEMBER many scenes and experiences
from my church mission trip to southern Peru in the first
decade of this century: the beautiful faces of the children
in the pueblo where we served, the women who bent to their
work in the field with small children colorfully strapped to
their backs, my first taste of maracuya fruit, and so much more.
My wife and I shared such experiences with about twenty others from the United States while providing simple dental clinics
and evangelistic efforts in and around Arequipa, Peru's second
most populous city. But the most memorable moment in that
trip belonged exclusively to me.

Our trip to Peru occurred in the midst of a grueling and
demoralizing season of ministry for me. I'd been leading our
church in Ohio through a construction project and a period of
rapid growth. We'd enjoyed many blessings and weathered many
storms together. But as my wife and I left home for ten days in
Peru, I was physically, emotionally, and spiritually exhausted. For
the first time in my adult life, I struggled with severe depression.
I gained weight from stress eating. My prayers rang hollow. My
health declined. I arrived in Peru feeling defeated, depleted, and
uncharacteristically fearful for the future.

There, however, I had a God moment, an experience with
parallels to an incident in the life of the patriarch Jacob on his

journey from Paddan-Aram back to his old neighborhood of Canaan. It's described in the thirty-second chapter of Genesis.

Many years earlier, Jacob had repeatedly wronged his twin brother, Esau, deceiving him and stealing one blessing after another from him before he ran away from home, found the love of his life, and prospered in wealth, possessions, and honor. But now, returning to his homeland with huge flocks of sheep and goats, great herds of camels, cattle, and donkeys, along with two wives, numerous servants, and eleven sons, Jacob must face the prospect of a reunion with his brother, Esau—a possibly awkward, even dangerous, reunion. All his wealth, all he had achieved—even his life and the lives of those he loves—could be taken from him if Esau decides to exact revenge. So, Jacob prays:

> O God of my father Abraham, God of my father Isaac, LORD, you who said to me, "Go back to your country and your relatives, and I will make you prosper," I am unworthy of all the kindness and faithfulness you have shown your servant. I had only my staff when I crossed this Jordan, but now I have become two camps. Save me, I pray, from the hand of my brother Esau, for I am afraid he will come and attack me, and also the mothers with their children." (Genesis 32:9–12, NIV)

After Jacob prays, he is still on edge. He's weary. Weak. Worried. So, he tries to hedge his bets, so to speak. He sends part of his caravan ahead, in separate groups, to buy Esau's favor before they ever meet. Next, he sends his family and remaining possessions along behind them, and camps alone overnight. At least that's what he thought. That's how he felt. But then, somehow, at some point, he is no longer alone:

So Jacob was left alone, and a man wrestled with him till daybreak. When the man saw that he could not overpower him, he touched the socket of Jacob's hip so that his hip was wrenched as he wrestled with the man. Then the man said, "Let me go, for it is daybreak."

But Jacob replied, "I will not let you go unless you bless me."

The man asked him, "What is your name?"

"Jacob," he answered.

Then the man said, "Your name will no longer be Jacob, but Israel, because you have struggled with God and with humans and have overcome."

Jacob said, "Please tell me your name."

But he replied, "Why do you ask my name?" Then he blessed him there.

So Jacob called the place Peniel, saying, "It is because I saw God face to face, and yet my life was spared."

The sun rose above him as he passed Peniel, and he was limping because of his hip.
(Genesis 32:24–31, NIV)

No wonder it's one of the most famous and fascinating accounts in the Bible. Not only because it was an important, name-changing, life-altering event in Jacob's life, but also because of the many ways that Jacob's story is my story too. And yours.

He Is with You
THE BIBLE tells us that when his entourage had all departed, Jacob was alone. But in the same line, we're told that he wasn't

alone: "So Jacob was left alone, and a man wrestled with him till daybreak" (Genesis 32:24, NIV).

There's so much worth noticing in that seeming paradox. The biblical writer didn't make a mistake. It's not a contradiction the editor should've caught. It's a fundamental reality of life.

Jacob's companions had all gone on ahead, and yet he was not alone. Another Companion was there and made Himself known. The Genesis account repeatedly refers to Jacob's visitor as "a man." Many years later, the prophet Hosea would write:

In the womb he [Jacob] grasped his brother's heel;
  as a man he struggled with God.
He struggled with the angel and overcame him;
  he wept and begged for his favor. (Hosea 12:3–4, NIV)

So, which was it? A man? An angel? God? By the end of his experience, Jacob apparently got a clear picture, calling the place *Peniel,* which means "face of God," because "I saw God face to face" (Genesis 32:30, NIV).

However lonely we may feel at times, we are not alone, "never, no, never alone."[1] A. W. Tozer wrote:

What now does the divine immanence mean in direct Christian experience? It means simply that God is here. Wherever we are, God is here. There is no place, there can be no place, where He is not. Ten million intelligences standing at as many points in space and separated by incomprehensible distances can each one say with equal truth, God is here. No point is nearer to God than any other point. It is exactly as near to God from any place as it is from any other place. No one is in mere distance any farther from or any nearer to God than any other person is.

These are truths believed by every instructed Christian. It remains for us to think on them and pray over them until they begin to glow with us.[2]

The testimony of Scripture makes it clear that God is omnipresent—that is, present everywhere—but God's Word also identifies our Lord as *Immanuel*, "God with us" (Isaiah 7:14; Matthew 1:23). We can believe the truth of God's constant presence, His immanence, His "with-us-ness." We can in faith receive what Jacob experienced.

He is with you . . . in your emotional lows.

He is with you . . . in your ecstatic highs.

He is with you . . . in your sadness and grief.

He is with you . . . in the doctor's office and the operating room.

He is with you . . . on your commute.

He is with you . . . in your sleepless nights.

He is with you . . . in the doctor's office.

He is with you . . . in the funeral home.

He is with you . . . in the grocery store.

He is with you . . . on the bus and on the train.

He is with you . . . in your sadness and grief.

He is with you . . . when you go out and when you come in.

He is with you . . . when you feel His presence and when you don't.

He is "with you always, to the very end of the age" (Matthew 28:20, NIV).

He Is for You

PERHAPS, LIKE ME, you've read the Bible account of Jacob wrestling with God many times. Many people have. Yet how many pause, not only to question how Jacob could be "alone" and "not alone" at the same time, but also to wonder why and how his wrestling match started.

The account begins so matter-of-factly that it's easy to let the wonder of it slip past us: "So Jacob was left alone, and a man wrestled with him till daybreak" (Genesis 32:24, NIV). We're not told how this happened.

Did Jacob wake from sleep and jump into a defensive posture? Is that how it started? Did Jacob suspect this "man" was a bandit? Did he assume his opponent was an assassin sent by his brother Esau? Was Jacob simply in the habit of challenging any man who came within a few feet of his camp?

We don't know. Maybe it's not important for us to know how and why it started, but simply to understand that Jacob, who must have thought he was alone for the night, encountered a Presence who grappled with him.

We also don't know at what point Jacob figured out that he was in the presence of God. Was it at some point as the contest wore on? Or when he was wounded? Was it when the man said, "Let me go, for it is daybreak"? Was it when Jacob said, "I will not let you go unless you bless me"? That sounds like he knew—or at least suspected—whom he was dealing with.

Amazingly, however, the account says, "When the man saw that he could not overpower him, he touched the socket of Jacob's hip" (Genesis 32:25, NIV). How is that possible? Almighty God contended with Jacob—and "could not overpower him"? What a statement!

We know that God is all-powerful. He "made the heavens and the earth by [His] great power and outstretched arm. Nothing is too hard for [Him]" (Jeremiah 32:17, NIV). "He changes times and seasons; he deposes kings and raises up others" (Daniel 2:21, NIV). How can Jacob, who is running from his father-in-law and afraid to meet his brother, wrestle God to a draw?

Perhaps the answer is this: God wasn't against Jacob; He was *for* him. God didn't overpower Jacob, because God wasn't an adversary; God was a sparring partner. He was on Jacob's side. And His purpose in wrestling Jacob wasn't to win but to bless.

The same is true for you. Whatever hurts you've suffered in the past, whatever misfortune has come your way, whatever abuse you've survived, betrayals you've endured, rejection you've felt, this you can know: God is *for* you (see Psalm 56:9). He is on your side (see Psalm 124:1–2). He is not your antagonist; He is your helper (see Psalm 118:7). The Lord Almighty is with you; the God of Jacob is your refuge (see Psalm 46:7, 11). And if God is *for* you, who can prevail against you (see Romans 8:31)?

He Is Changing You

JACOB THOUGHT he was alone, but he wasn't. He wrestled with a man who wasn't a mere man. And he didn't lose the match, but he limped away from it. The Bible says, "When the man saw that he could not overpower him, he touched the socket of Jacob's hip so that his hip was wrenched as he wrestled with the man" (Genesis 32:25, NIV).

Jacob's encounter with God changed him. When all was said and done, the Bible says, "The sun rose above him as he passed Peniel, and he was limping because of his hip" (Genesis 32:31, NIV).

He would go on to meet his brother Esau in weakness rather than strength. He approached Esau limping, wounded. As it turned out, Esau welcomed his prodigal brother with open arms. . . but it may have turned out differently if Jacob had not approached him, limping, in humble awareness of his weakness. As God would tell another of His servants, many years later, "My power is made perfect in weakness" (2 Corinthians 12:9, NIV).

God's presence and power in Jacob's life changed more than his stride. Their all-night scuffle resulted in another change. God said, "Your name will no longer be Jacob, but Israel, because you have struggled with God and with humans and have overcome" (Genesis 32:28, NIV). The "con man" had become a champion.

God's presence is often comforting and strengthening—but not always. It may sometimes seem as though God is wrestling with you. You may find His moves surprising, even baffling. He may seem to be stretching you, challenging you, even hindering you. God is always working in your life, but you may not always feel comfortable as He does. But you can always be confident that His touch is changing you.

God's touch may make you leap with joy and energy, or it may give you a limp, as it did for Jacob. His touch may reach deep within you and give you a new identity, as it did for Jacob. His touch may open your eyes and fill you with compassion, may lift up your head and encourage you in a moment of crisis, or may impart new strength and prepare your hands for a fresh challenge.

In Jacob's case, God's presence and power prepared Him for the coming day, when he would face an uncertain situation and begin a new chapter in life. In your case, God may change you or your circumstances. He may change your understanding or your perspective. He may answer your prayers as you hope—or answer them in ways you could never have foreseen. But you can be confident of this: By His presence in your life, "he who began a good work in you will carry it on to completion until the day of Christ Jesus" (Philippians 1:6, NIV).

He Changed Me

MY "PENIEL MOMENT" was a Sunday evening service in the church that was the base of operations for my wife's and my mission trip in Peru. People of all ages filed in from the pueblo and sat on benches in the simple chapel. They sang along enthusiastically with recorded worship music that streamed through loudspeakers. The words, of course, were in Spanish, but I sang along as well as I could. I remember standing to my feet and finding an out-of-the-way corner in the chapel, where I could be "alone" but "not alone." I sensed intensifying emotion in the room as the congregation sang, "Dios manda lluvia"—*God, send rain.* "Derrama de tu Espíritu" —*Pour out Your Spirit.*

I don't recall the other words in that song, but I sang along, understanding only parts of the syllables I sang. I closed my eyes. I tensed. I began to wrestle with God. I pushed, He pushed back. Tears streamed down my face. I felt broken and wounded, and when the worship service ended, I sat for a long time on one of the benches in that chapel. Nothing had changed, and everything had changed. I limped from that service, changed, humbled, renewed, and strengthened—and ready for a new season of following and serving Jesus.

The stories in the coming pages of this book relate how God works through ordinary people in extraordinary ways—

"chance" encounters that changed a life, miraculous examples of God's timing, striking stories of emotional and physical healing, and more. The accounts come from all sorts of people in all kinds of places, but they're joined together by the awareness that God is always and everywhere present in our lives—with us, for us, changing us—and strengthening us by His touch. I hope these pages will remind you of or awaken you to your own "Peniel moment"—an awareness of God's constant presence and experience of His strengthening touch.

Endnotes
1. Ludie Carrington Day Pickett, "Never Alone," public domain.
2. A. W. Tozer, *The Pursuit of God* (Minneapolis: Bethany House Publishers, 2014), 62–63.

God is not calling you to rush through the life He has given you. You are not just randomly going from moment to moment and year to year like an arrow loosely aimed into the wilderness. Every day matters. God does everything with an intentional plan and purpose.

—Morgan Harper Nichols, artist and writer

CHAPTER 1

Occurrences with Divine Timing

A Voice in the Snow

By Kate Finlay

I threw off the blankets, grabbed my robe, and dashed to the bedroom door.

"Kate! Where are you going?"

I didn't answer, just kept running down the darkened hall into the living room. As I ran toward the kitchen, I bashed my shin on a table. It just added to the flow of tears.

Alan called from the bedroom, "I'm sorry. Come back."

Sorry. I'd heard that before. I barreled through the back door into the yard, then closed it gently, making sure to not lock it. How I wished I could slam it. Make it shake on its hinges like I shook when Alan slammed his fist into the wall.

I tiptoed through the slushy snow and climbed atop our wooden picnic table, plunking my slippered feet on the bench. Dropping my face into my hands, I let the sobs loose. *How can this be happening? God, I'm really trying. What does he want from me?* I cried and railed. *Can't You stop his rages? Why did he marry me if he doesn't want me around?*

I shivered, then wrapped my robe tighter around me and peered over my shoulder. Checking. Hoping. Hoping he'd follow me, hoping he wouldn't. Hoping a still-dark house meant the kids had slept through this.

God, why did You let us marry? I asked so many times if we should. Why didn't You make Your "no" crystal clear?

I had been a single mom, the sole support of my nine-year-old son. After many lean years I was finally working at a job I loved and earning enough to take care of us. I was happy. My son was happy.

When I met Alan and noticed a mutual attraction, I begged God to remove this man from my heart and my life. I didn't need complications, and it seemed Alan didn't, either. He was a widower raising three teenagers—plenty of challenges for a single dad without adding more.

Our courtship held no hint of the problems I now faced. After the honeymoon, we moved into Alan's bungalow, and I worked hard to be a good wife and stepmother, while not letting my son get lost in this larger family.

I rotated cooking their favorite dinners, made four

> **"For I know the plans I have for you," says the LORD. "They are plans for good and not for disaster, to give you a future and a hope."**
>
> —JEREMIAH 29:11 (NLT)

different types of lunches—with or without mustard, with cheese, without cheese, with extra cheese, one peanut butter and jelly. I had Alan's coffee ready when he dragged in from work, and I tried to hold off for half an hour before sharing any bad news about grades or the ever-present requests for money and rides. I knew he appreciated it; he told me so. He was surprised and thankful for the garden we planted, the walls I painted, and the gallery of kids' awards I hung in the hall.

Though we neared our one-year anniversary, I still considered myself a newlywed. And when he hugged me, everything seemed right with the world.

So his unprovoked outbursts of rage stunned and terrified me. They rocked the foundation of our home. I never knew how to protect our world from angry words and flying fists. Never knew how to prevent them. And I hadn't learned how to inoculate my heart against them either. So this night, as I had slid into bed, cuddled with him, and begun to talk, I was expecting many things—but not being pushed aside while he punched a hole in the wall next to our bed.

The LORD himself will fight for you. Just stay calm.

—EXODUS 14:14 (NLT)

Sitting on the damp table, I cynically told myself I was fortunate the wall, not my face, was at the end of his fist. Tonight he was obviously trying to *not* hurt me.

I doubled over and wept again. "God," I whispered. "Doesn't he *know* his rage shreds my heart? That it threatens our home even if he doesn't hit me?"

My misery spawned a litany of questions—without answers. *Why does he do it? What did I do to provoke him? What can I do to stop this?* And the most agonizing: *How can I endure this?*

The questions hung in the frigid dark like the puffs of my frosty breath, and hope dripped to the ground along with my tears.

Eventually exhaustion crept over me, and I couldn't stop shivering. I couldn't force more questions or more tears. An emptiness blacker than the cold night wrapped around me as I tried to fight off resignation that this was my lot: Fear. Frustration. Isolation. All I could see ahead was day after bleak day strung together until life ebbed away.

Years earlier I had memorized verses that reminded me that God leads me through the valleys, He is my Light and Salvation, and with Him I have nothing to fear. I had viewed challenges as opportunities for God to show up in mighty ways. And He had!

Where was He now?

I sighed and watched the vapor cloud drift heavenward. As it dissipated, stars twinkled against the black sky. *Please, God. I know You're there. Please. Do something.*

I sat upright, preparing to trudge back into the house, hoping Alan was asleep and I could soon follow. "God, I'm so lonely. More than the nights I spent alone after tucking my son into bed. Worse than when I sat alone in a church service on Valentine's Day, surrounded by couples celebrating by standing together, speaking vows to each other. But I can't endure this. I feel like I'm shriveling up until I just die."

The word rattled around my brain. *Die. Die.* It intensified. *Die!*

My mind toyed with the idea of relieving my pain and confusion this way. But I knew that was not God's message to me. I tried one more time.

"Please, won't You make Alan quit the rages, open up, and talk with me? I can't stand the loneliness." I crumpled over, crying again. "Please, God. I want him to *want* to be with me."

And, as if I'd heard a voice from someone standing at my shoulder, God whispered to my heart. *I know what it is like, dear child, to desire a loved one to seek you out and spend time with you only.*

"You do?" I waited.

GOD'S GIFT OF SIGHT
— By Tez Brooks —

WHEN STUDENTS IMMERSE themselves in recreation, teachers often try whispering to get their attention. Raising their voice doesn't help—kids don't hear it. A quiet tone causes kids to close their mouths and zero in on what adults are saying. Only then can they hear instruction or encouragement. The distraction of activity is immense for anyone. Even honorable deeds can overpower the Lord's call as He whispers, "Come and sit at my feet." God's voice is much clearer when people disconnect from emails, television, radio, and other distractions.

Yes. I hurt each time I call to you and you refuse.

Shame heated my cheeks as I realized how often God had invited me to come away and spend time just with Him, but I had handed out the same cold shoulder that Alan had wounded me with. I was a busy mom and had plenty of excuses: shopping, mopping, driving, homework. I talked with my Lord—but always on the move. If He wanted to trail after me as I bustled through my duties, I was happy to have Him tag along. But like so many busy moms with a toddler who's always *there*, I seldom stopped and gave God my focused attention.

Yes, my Lord understood my sorrow. *I'm sorry. So sorry. Please forgive me.*

Like being wrapped in a warm blanket, the blessing of God's forgiveness enfolded me. Then He nudged again. *Now, forgive Alan.*

Forgive Alan? Yes, from the security and comfort of fellowship with God, I felt that I could extend forgiveness to my husband.

And over the years, as I grew to know God better and let Him lead me, He graciously and repeatedly comforted my heart and changed my life. Gradually the times of disappointment over Alan's distance hurt less because I gave them to God and gave patience to Alan. In response, God rained encouragement over me. And as an extra blessing, He slowly, but as clearly as a sunrise shatters the night, drew Alan into close fellowship and enabled him to become the husband and father who blesses our family today.

Silence Surrounded by Chaos

By Constance Gilbert

My first brand-new car was a 1977 blue Dodge Colt with a manual transmission. I learned how to shift and practiced in an empty parking lot. After thirty minutes, my impatient teacher, my brother, got out of the car saying, "You're on your own. If you want to go anywhere, you'll have to shift without stalling it all the time."

He grinned and walked home.

As my timing and coordination improved over the next week or so, my frustration decreased. I could no longer refer to the Colt as *it* or *the car*. After all, we had bonded through all those starts, stalls, and jerks. I named it Charlie.

On December 31, 1979, at 7:30 a.m., life changed for Charlie and me.

Traffic was lighter than usual as I headed for work. Charlie's engine purred quietly as I hummed, waiting for the light to change. Suddenly, a full-size Buick turned into oncoming traffic. It hit a brown station wagon, shoving it through the intersection toward the curb. I sighed with relief as I watched the other drivers swerve, avoiding additional collisions.

Then...

Gasping, I tightened my grip on the steering wheel. That big old Buick was heading straight toward Charlie.

I'm going to die! Who will take care of my son? I can't even say goodbye to him. Should I keep the brakes on? I closed my eyes.

I leaned back against my seat and braced for the impact that would surely lead to my death and send faithful Charlie to the junkyard.

I felt the impact but never heard the crash. All was silent.

I don't hurt. I must be dead.

I opened my eyes. The traffic was flowing as usual, but I couldn't hear it. The windshield and dashboard were intact and so was I—no breathing problems, no pain, no bleeding, and no sound.

Then out of the silence came a whisper. "Have no fear. *You* will raise your son."

The street sounds returned a few moments later. I sat, letting the words register. I'd been widowed when my son was only two years old, so the relief that he wouldn't be orphaned was palpable.

I was shaking and my legs were wobbly as I slowly stepped out of Charlie. The young driver of the station wagon ran up to me. "I'm so sorry. Are you hurt?" Assured that I was OK, he ran, calling over his shoulder, "I'll call the police."

Meanwhile, the Buick driver stood by his door, cussing and shifting his body back and forth as if to keep his balance. This older man accused me of ruining his New Year's Eve, which

> I thank God for you—the God I serve with a clear conscience, just as my ancestors did. Night and day I constantly remember you in my prayers.
>
> —2 TIMOTHY 1:3 (NLT)

was still hours away. He never asked if I was hurt and instead continued to hurl profanities at me.

The young driver returned and tried to apologize again until I firmly told him, "I'm fine and you did not cause the accident! Do you understand? You did *not* cause this. He hit you. Then me."

The Buick driver was still swearing and blaming both of us as the police car pulled up. The officer checked all of us for injuries, then scanned the scene.

"Were there any other vehicles involved? Who was driving the Colt? OK, let's take a look at the station wagon."

When the officer returned, he asked, "Ma'am, am I right in assuming you were sitting here, while the light was red, and saw the initial accident?"

> **For God saved us and called us to live a holy life. He did this, not because we deserved it, but because that was his plan from before the beginning of time— to show us his grace through Christ Jesus.**
>
> —2 TIMOTHY 1:9 (NLT)

I nodded, but I was still shaking. I braced myself against my car. Charlie was holding me up.

"You're sure you aren't hurt?"

I nodded again.

"OK, let's see if we can get these vehicles off the road. Then we'll write this up."

He walked around to poor Charlie's other side, assessing the damage. Then he looked back at me, shaking his head, "Ma'am, how did you survive this? Your engine should have ended up in your lap!"

Charlie's front end was inside the Buick's grille. With the young driver's help, the officer managed to separate the cars. The only damage to Charlie was a broken headlight, a twisted bumper, and a bent fender. Once that fender was pulled off Charlie's tire, I parked nearby in a parking lot.

The Buick had a broken front end and coolant wept onto the pavement. The men pushed it to the curb to await a tow truck. The yellow caution signs in place, the policeman asked us to get in the squad car. Men in the back seat.

All this time, Mr. Profanity continued spewing nasty words and accusations, even in the back seat of the squad car.

I sat in the front as the officer questioned me and filled out the necessary report.

"I saw your car, yet I still can't believe it. The skid marks show he didn't brake until 6 feet from you. The impact alone…well, I'm amazed you're not dead or severely injured."

I smiled. "My guardian angel was on the hood. I have more to do before I die."

The policeman looked puzzled. He stared at me for a moment, then gave me a nod with a slight smile.

Mr. Profanity was cited for causing the accident. His tirade escalated.

The cop scowled as he turned toward the back seat. His compassion had flipped to confrontation. "Sir, I have asked you repeatedly to be quiet. If you aren't, I will be writing additional citations." The barrage of nastiness continued under the old man's breath.

Afterward, when I headed toward my car, the insults still poured out from the back seat. "You've ruined my New Year's Eve!"

Now his speech was slurred, and he sounded out of control. It seemed he had been celebrating too early, so he was going to end one year and begin another in jail for drinking and driving.

Looking back, I know Charlie was indeed inside and under the hood of that Buick. I know two things cannot occupy the same place at the same time Therefore, I cannot explain what I saw. More important, I still have no doubts that my guardian angel protected me. I never had even a bruise.

God used a potential tragedy to erase my fears about what would happen to my son if I died. I had promised to raise him like Hannah raised Samuel—to serve the Lord. I knew then that I would be able to fulfill that promise. And I did.

Today, nearly forty years later, my son is the father of three. He co-owns a graphic design company where he creates covers for Christian books, and he has also gone on several short-term mission trips. He is active in his church, community, and the children's school.

Oh, and Charlie? He became my son's first car.

Praise Precedes Miracles

By Dianna L. Lanser

"Thanksgiving always precedes the miracle." I found this quote from Ann Voskamp to be brilliantly true during an unexpected season of change my family experienced.

Wanting to free himself from a toxic environment, my husband, Brent, resigned from his role as a landscape designer and architect. I knew his work situation was unbearable, but Brent had promised me that he would find a new position before he stepped away.

So, when he came home from work one evening and told me he'd quit his job, I can't say that I was understanding. Instead, I was shocked and angry and felt betrayed.

Then, in short order, fear and doubt showed up and slipped through the wooden gate of my heart. What if Brent couldn't secure a new position right away? Would we have to put a hold on the kids' plans and activities? What if we couldn't pay our mortgage and the rest of our monthly bills? Would we eventually lose our house?

For the sake of keeping peace in the home, I stuffed my anger and worry and did my best to carry on with some semblance of faith. After all, God had brought our family through times of financial shortage before; He could do it again.

Thankfully, Brent found a part-time position right away, and then he got busy networking with others in the landscaping field. He also asked his uncle to mentor him through the job search process. These small steps forward pumped up my deflated heart and allowed me to go about the business of managing the home with a greater sense of hope.

I occupied my mind and free time moving our oldest daughter into her new off-campus college apartment and visiting potential universities and filling out financial aid forms with our high school senior. And then there was our sixteen-year-old, whom we were easing into the driver's seat. At the same time, we were running our two middle schoolers to and from after-school and evening activities.

With Brent's part-time job being thirty-five minutes from home and mine twenty minutes away, we did *a lot* of driving. This wouldn't have been so bad, but our second vehicle—Brent's vehicle—was an older, gas-guzzling Suburban, and gasoline prices had reached four dollars a gallon that January!

Our primary vehicle, a 2000 Toyota Camry, was perfect in every way except that the dome light didn't work. We had tried installing new bulbs (a couple of times), jiggling wires, and checking fuses, but our backyard mechanical skills had kept us in the dark since summer.

Because daylight is rationed during Michigan winters and only available between the hours of 8:00 a.m. and 5:00 p.m., a working dome light is essential for families with school-aged kids. Those tiny, ten-watt bulbs allow homework-laden kids to use the fifteen-minute drive home from play practice or the thirty-minute stop for groceries to study for a test or complete a math problem or two.

While we didn't have the luxury of a working dome light, we still loved our trusty Camry. We decided to sell the Suburban and replace it with another fuel-efficient Camry.

Despite gas prices being at an all-time high, miraculously our beautiful Suburban sold quickly, and the very next day, my husband found a clean 1998 Camry about an hour north from where we lived. After dinner that evening, we drove the sixty miles to pick up and welcome our new/old Camry into the family. Even though Brent offered me the opportunity to drive it home, I felt more comfortable driving the vehicle I loved and knew so well.

For two weeks, when my stress was at its peak, I'd been trying to take the words of 1 Thessalonians 5:18 (NIV) to heart: "Give thanks in all circumstances; for this is God's will for you in Christ Jesus." I took this to mean God wanted me to give thanks when life is hard, when money is short, when I'm scared, and when I don't always see eye to eye with my husband. And now, without consciously thanking God and despite my mustard seed–sized faith, He had graciously provided a buyer for our Suburban and provided a great economy car to get us through this time of wondering and waiting.

> **Oh, give thanks to the LORD, for he is good; for his steadfast love endures forever!**
>
> —1 CHRONICLES 16:34 (ESV)

So, driving home on south US 131, my heart was overflowing. Praise and thanksgiving poured from my lips, and like a breath's vapor rises in the cold, I lifted my offering of gratitude to the Creator God.

"Thank You, Father, for this beautiful full moon. The heavens declare Your glory, the skies proclaim the work of Your hands! Thank You for providing a new/old Camry. Thank You for providing a buyer for the Suburban. God, You are so good! You are the Giver of every good and perfect gift. You are worthy of all my praise! Thank You for my husband, our kids, for our good health, for our warm, cozy house. And Lord, it would be so cool if you could fix the dome light…"

I don't know where that request came from or why I asked such a silly, random thing, but the minute the words left my lips, the dome light that hadn't worked for at least seven months suddenly illuminated the inside of the car with golden light—all by itself! The God who loves me saw me! He heard me! And in His goodness, He showed up and gifted me with a personal parting of the Red Sea, a serving of manna, a solid rock monument of remembrance.

> **Every day I will praise you and extol your name for ever and ever.**
>
> —PSALM 145:2 (NIV)

When I could have been worried and distracted by all the losses we potentially faced, I was moved to count the blessings God had given us. And in that moment of counting, God split the darkness with the glorious brightness of that old broken dome light and showed me I could count on him.

In the following weeks, my husband continued to make phone calls, knock on doors, and meet with acquaintances in his line of work. The Lord again provided. Just before the first signs of spring, when Michiganders come out of their sleepy cocoons and begin to clamor for a spot in line for a landscape design, Brent accepted a position at a long-established company, helping to build their landscaping division.

GOD'S GIFT OF TOUCH
— By Eryn Lynum —

THERE IS A peculiar temperature shift in the rare instance of a solar eclipse. As the moon slips between the earth and sun, obscuring light and ushering in a false night during daytime hours, an eerie chill is cast over the landscape. What feels supernatural is, in reality, completely natural. A total eclipse of the sun is a matter of mathematics and science—entirely predictable by measurements God created in the universe. With skin goose-bumped by the frigidity of an eclipse breeze, it is wise to remember God's power. Even when circumstances feel out of control, God is completely sovereign. He is a God of reason.

Now, whenever I find myself in a time of loss, sickness, shortage, or waiting, I remember the dome light miracle, and, instead of becoming afraid or worried, I try to thank the Lord for His faithfulness, His goodness, and His providence. And even though I've never again received a fantastical, unbelievable miracle like I did that clear winter night, a miracle always happens inside me. I'm gifted with the knowledge of God's presence. I'm filled with His peace, comfort, and the joy-filled power of praise and gratitude.

Following His Lead

By Kelly J. Stigliano

"I'm just getting this *now*?"

My husband, Jerry, jumped at my screech, spilling his coffee. From his lanky 6-foot elevation, the hot brew splattered across the floor. He grabbed a paper towel and leaned down to wipe it up, nearly bumping his balding head on the countertop.

"What?" He tried to conceal his annoyance. "What is that?"

I handed him the opened envelope with the crumpled paper sticking out. "This! This just came in the mail."

"Mm-hmm." His indifference told me he hadn't thoroughly read the announcement. "It's an invitation to your twenty-five-year high school class reunion. You like these things, don't you?"

"Yes! That's the problem. Look at the date!"

Angst and insecurities from the past tried to splash up on my well-fought-for adult self-confidence. Memories of the jocks, brains, heads, and introverts came to mind. I hadn't completely fit in with any of them in those days. At our small northeastern Ohio school, most students were friendly, but I considered few to be close friends. Still, I had enjoyed chatting with everyone at previous class reunions and hated to be left out.

"Oh my." Now he was getting it. "That's next weekend! Did you see this little note attached to the invitation?"

I snatched it out of his hand. "What note?"

The yellow sticky note had a message in red ink. "We didn't have your current address and finally tracked you down via your aunt. I hope this makes it to you in time and that you'll be able to join us."

"Oh." Feeling contrite, I calmed down. "Well, shoot. We moved and I guess they simply didn't know." I enjoyed a brief moment of respect, imagining them trying to locate me. "I'll see if I can find a flight at a decent price." Off I ran to the computer.

To be fair, keeping up with our whereabouts probably wasn't easy. Although I'd stayed in northeastern Ohio following high school graduation, after I remarried in 1985, we'd moved to five different states for Jerry's job. My graduating class had a reunion every five years. When we moved to Florida, we finally "fell through the cracks." I was glad they had asked my aunt where I lived.

If you remain in me and my words remain in you, ask whatever you wish, and it will be done for you.

—JOHN 15:7 (NIV)

I found a last-minute airfare website, clicked the "flight and car combo" tab, and entered my departure and arrival cities. I couldn't believe my eyes.

"Jerry! Come look at this."

The dates, times, airports, and even automobile options were perfect. I reread the package price.

"Does that really say $125?" He was skeptical. "That can't possibly include car rental."

"Well, let me check again." I dug deeper and it did, indeed, include airfare and car rental for four days. That was an incredible price, even in 2003!

Jerry had to work that weekend, so I would attend alone. "You can stay with my parents," he said. Dom and Eva lived thirty minutes from the restaurant hosting the event.

I squealed, "I'm booking it!" Jerry agreed.

> **All this is for your benefit, so that the grace that is reaching more and more people may cause thanksgiving to overflow to the glory of God.**
>
> —2 CORINTHIANS 4:15 (NIV)

The following week, I packed my suitcase and prayed that God would show me His plan. I'd traveled alone before, but this was so rushed. I prayed for peace. Throughout the week I rejoiced that I would have an opportunity to see old friends and my in-laws. I thanked my Heavenly Father for the unbelievable price. I asked Him to be my divine traveling companion.

My ongoing conversation with our Lord reminded me of 1 Thessalonians 5:16–18 (ESV), which says, "Rejoice always, pray without ceasing, give thanks in all circumstances; for this is the will of God in Christ Jesus for you." I truly was celebrating.

Then we heard the news. Our dear friends in Ohio had suffered a terrible motorcycle accident. While they were traveling a country road, a van had pulled into their path, and they slammed into the side of the vehicle.

Both friends were injured, but Beth was hurt the worst. Her husband, Dan, was able to call her daughters and talk to the paramedics when they arrived with the ambulance. They took Beth to the Cleveland Clinic.

Our prayers took a detour. We fervently declared that she would recover and asked God for a total healing. We had faith as described in Hebrews 11:1 (NIV): "Now faith is confidence in what we hope for and assurance about what we do not see." We knew in our hearts Beth would recover.

The thought of visiting them while in Ohio briefly crossed my mind. I brushed it off, thinking out loud. "This is a family tragedy. I doubt they would appreciate a visitor in the middle of their crisis." Besides, the idea of driving into Cleveland was daunting. But God had planted a seed in my spirit.

As I traveled to Ohio for my class reunion, I had an unexplainable joy in my heart. I felt Christ's presence with me, boosting my confidence as I navigated the journey.

The flight was uneventful, and the rental car was a new Mercury Sable. "Come on, Jesus. Let's go see Dom and Eva!" I exclaimed as I put the key in the ignition.

My in-laws warmly welcomed me and helped me settle in. Our conversation was enjoyable, and our time together was special.

Normally I didn't like traveling at night, especially on long-forgotten roads. Driving to the reunion Saturday evening, however, I had no trouble seeing or traversing along the dark country byways. I was excited to go!

Seeing former classmates at the reunion was fun, but it felt like something was not complete. Returning home that night, after a brief chat with my in-laws, I excused myself to go to bed. I prayed, "Lord, this reunion was the reason I came here.

You gave me an unbelievable price so I could come. I loved seeing old friends, but, still, I feel like I have unfinished business here. What am I missing?"

The seed God previously planted began to sprout. I thought of visiting Beth and Dan. Within seconds I knew I was to drive to Cleveland to see my friends at the hospital. Although I hadn't driven into the city in years, I planned to make the trip Sunday. I slept well that night.

The next morning the sun was shining as I hopped into my rental car. "OK, Lord. Let's go!"

Because the car had no GPS, I was armed with a list of the routes I'd scoped out on a map. Normally I would be nervous, but, uncharacteristically, I sped off without concern, completely enjoying the journey with my Lord.

The hour-long drive flew by. At the hospital, I parked and entered the labyrinth that is the Cleveland Clinic. God seemed to be guiding me with His divine GPS.

Somehow, I found the correct level. As I walked through a waiting room, I saw Dan pacing the floor. Beth's middle daughter, Samantha, sat in a chair. I hadn't seen her in years.

Dan answered his cell phone as Samantha rose to greet me. She pointed out her son, a teenager sitting across the room. I pictured pages flying off a calendar because, in my mind, she was still a teenager.

She gave me an update on Beth as Dan updated his caller.

In my spirit I felt the pieces falling into place. This was exactly why I had come. My ongoing mental conversation with God ramped up as I prayed for this precious family.

I couldn't see Beth because she was in surgery. The doctors were putting titanium rods in her leg and arm. She chose not to have surgery on her jaw, opting instead to eat no solid food for a month. For her broken back, she opted for six months in a body brace. Her recovery would be difficult.

As I hugged Dan and Samantha, I felt the love of Christ pass from me to them. When I left, walking through the network of halls and floors, I continued my conversation with Christ, whispering, "Lord, this is why I'm here, isn't it?"

Although I didn't get to see Beth, I knew in my heart that what I'd done was enough. My job was complete.

"It's about obedience, isn't it?" I said to God. "Thank You for giving me the opportunity to come. Thank You for navigating me here on the road and through this building."

As I drove out onto the highway to head back to Dom and Eva's house, I couldn't help but smile. I kept saying, "Thank You, Lord. Nothing feels as good as obedience to You. Thank You for taking care of every detail as only You can do. You truly are remarkable!"

With my whirlwind weekend behind me, I basked in the love of God and the satisfaction received in obeying His loving guidance.

Nothing to Fear
in God's Hands

By Cheryl Anderson Davis

I can pinpoint the exact moment my family stopped going to church.

There was no casual drifting away. There was an abrupt end to formal, religious observance of the Sabbath in our household.

My parents had regularly attended services until I was six years old. My brother and sisters had all been baptized on schedule—once a child hit a certain age, it was time to make a commitment. When I turned six years old, my father became convinced I needed to be baptized.

My father did not listen to my mother's argument that I was terrified of water and that baptism by submersion for a very young child was not a good idea. I had almost drowned when I was four years old, resulting in my fear of water. My mother wanted to wait until I was a little older before requesting baptism.

But my father insisted that it was time for me to be baptized. When I went in front of the church, I panicked. I started to struggle and wanted to run away. I had no idea what baptism really meant. All I could think of were those Sunday school stories about how Abraham had almost sacrificed his son Isaac on an altar.

My father continued to insist that I be baptized. The pastor had to intervene. The deacons also got involved. Apparently, there was quite a scene. Ultimately, I was not baptized. And my family stopped attending that church—or any church.

As I a teenager I had the feeling I was running away from something. Driven by my hunger to resolve nagging spiritual questions, I visited numerous churches with friends. Eventually I accepted the Lord into my heart, but I only attended church services on a regular basis after I married. I wanted my children to grow up in a church. I wanted them to have mentors and godly people to teach them the basic tenents of God's Word—something I struggled to comprehend.

Then my sons asked to be baptized. They wondered why I had never been baptized. Excuses seemed hollow and lame.

> **Do not be afraid; do not be discouraged, for the LORD your God will be with you wherever you go.**
>
> —JOSHUA 1:9 (NIV)

I was thirty-nine years old. Something felt "undone." I knew I needed to make a public profession of my faith. I could have settled by just being sprinkled, but it seemed cowardly not to be baptized by submersion. However, I was still that little girl cringing inside…still terrified of water.

But I stepped out in faith and requested to be baptized.

I decided to take a hands-on approach to the problem. I practiced putting my head under water in the bathtub. That did not help. In fact, I just grew more apprehensive. I could never get my head below water level. As the scheduled date of my baptism grew closer, I grew extremely afraid I was going to panic and embarrass myself in front of another church congregation.

> **When you pass through the waters, I will be with you; and when you pass through the rivers, they will not sweep over you.**
>
> —ISAIAH 43:2 (NIV)

The morning I was finally baptized is very vivid in my memory. Jaw set with determination, I grudgingly trudged into the baptistry dressing room and donned my white robe. I was going to do this—force myself to be firm and unflinching. Fists clenched in my resolve, I would be the epitome of the Christian soldier marching as to war. I drew strength from the scripture 1 Timothy 6:12 (NIV): "Fight the good fight of the faith. Take hold of the eternal life to which you were called when you made your good confession in the presence of many witnesses."

But I was not the only person who was going to be baptized that dazzlingly brilliant Sunday morning. A young boy who was around nine years old joined me backstage. The associate pastor who was going to perform the rite of baptism introduced me to my fellow initiate into the Christian faith.

I don't remember the boy's name. In fact, I never recall our paths crossing again in the hallways of our megachurch. I know it is a ridiculous notion, but sometimes I wonder if this excited boy, his eyes aglow with enthusiasm, truly existed. His joy was unbounded—almost surreal—as if he had been asked to attend the best party ever. He begged to go first. Smiling, bare feet bouncing on the carpeted floor. Ecstatic.

And here I was, dreading the moment like a criminal awaiting execution.

One dunk. Done. The boy did a jig as he danced up the stairs on the far side of the baptistry.

My turn.

Strange how life-changing events are often suspended in the ether of memory. They're like grainy, aged snapshots you review later in life and wonder if such an event truly happened to you.

I will never be able to explain how the fear and trepidation completely lifted off my bent shoulders and did not accompany me down the stairs into the baptistry font. Maybe because at that moment I was not a scared little girl facing the test of my faith alone. Something, or someone, stood beside with me at the height of my fear. It was almost as if a protective bubble engulfed me. I cannot recall my head going under water. I experienced no gagging, no thrashing about, no panic.

I was elated. Not because my ordeal was over and not because I had not embarrassed myself in front of the congregation. I knew something amazing had occurred. And I was extremely grateful. Like the innocent little boy, I, too, danced up the stairs on the far side of baptistry.

I continued to dance with joy as I changed clothes in the dressing room. I still recall standing in front of a mirror, hairbrush in hand, marveling that my hair was wet and not having any recollection of how that had happened.

I am still afraid of water. I will never jump into a swimming pool. I cannot force my head below the water in the bathtub, but I don't have to worry about overcoming that fear. I over-

GOD'S GIFT OF TOUCH
— By Tez Brooks —

WHETHER ROSE PETALS or kittens, sandpaper or hot coals—the Creator wanted humankind to experience His creation intimately. So, the skin contains several types of touch receptors. Some parts of the body have more receptors than others. For instance, fingers are more sensitive than the shoulders and back. When touching something (hot, cold, pain, or pressure), the touch receptors speed information to the brain. The brain receives the signal and reports how something feels, so the person knows to pull away or pause and enjoy the sensation. The sense of touch is a precious but underappreciated gift from God.

---

came a worse terror when I made my confession of faith before many witnesses. And I did not have to face that challenge on my own power.

I believe there was a reason the wait was long before I was baptized. Perhaps I had to learn there is nothing to fear when I put myself in God's hands and realize His presence goes with me in every fearful situation—even if it's into a baptistry.

Miracle on Wildcat Mountain

By Janet Sady

When I came to my senses, I realized that I was lying in a crevice between two large boulders, looking up at the sky, which was visible between the treetops. I was crying and pleading with God.

Earlier that morning, the mist had given way to blue New England skies. White fluffy clouds drifted by as we drove up Route 16 to Pinkham Notch, New Hampshire. My husband, Frank, and I had hiked the Jackson Mountain Trail as part of the Appalachian Trail the previous day. We stopped short of our goal because of a rushing mountain stream over which we needed to cross. Snow melt from Mt. Washington had turned the docile little stream into a raging torrent.

We noticed on our map that the Appalachian Trail continued on the other side of Route 16, and that was our goal today.

Frank and I are seventy-six years old. He keeps active by playing golf three times a week. I, on the other hand, spend a lot of time on the computer, though I do go out for walks as often as possible. After scaling Black Cap Mountain and tackling several other hikes a couple of days before, I felt ready. The trails were through the woods, up hills, and were filled with boulder-strewn gullies and bare roots. Sometimes we also had to cross small streams.

As we started on the trail to Lost Pond, I observed many rocks and huge boulders we would have to climb over. We maneuvered with our hiking poles. In between the boulders were pools of leaves, mud, and water. The trail ran parallel to the river, and we soon found the dammed-up area known as Lost Pond.

The trail became even more difficult after the Pond with some boulders reaching almost 8 feet high. We picked our way around and between them. Because of the height of the boulders, I couldn't see Frank, who was several yards ahead of me. I planted my walking stick in a small crevice and proceeded to step between two wide boulders.

> **For He shall give His angels charge over thee, to keep thee in all thy ways. They shall bear thee up in their hands, lest thou dash thy foot against a stone.**
>
> —PSALM 91:11–12 (KJV)

The fall happened so quickly that I didn't realize I was falling or have time to call out to Frank. A few seconds later, I made contact with the ground,

The crevice was large enough to accommodate my body, and it was full of wet, soft leaves. I began crying out to God. All I could think of was broken bones and how far we had hiked from the beginning of the trail. I asked God to please not allow me to have serious injuries.

When I finished my petition for God's intervention, I looked to my right and there, folded neatly beside me, were my glasses and walking stick. It was just as if I decided to take a nap, removed them, and laid them down.

I retrieved my glasses and put them on. Then I took stock of my body in an attempt to ascertain the extent of my injuries.

But as I took stock of my body, with wonder, I began to take stock of miracles too.

At this time, Frank came back looking for me when he did not see me coming behind him. He was shocked to see me lying there. We checked for injuries.

Blood ran from my knuckles, and my head and my knee hurt. I was lying in a narrow crevice between two giant boulders. The space miraculously was just wide enough for my body to fit. I am certain the Lord guided the fall exactly straight down.

I had lost consciousness for several seconds. If I had been conscious, I would have tried to prevent the fall, and I am sure would have been more seriously injured. I became aware that I was falling just before my head came in contact with a small outcropping of rock at the base of the boulders.

> **I will lift up mine eyes unto the hills, from whence cometh my help. My help cometh from the LORD, which made heaven and earth. He will not suffer thy foot to be moved; he that keepeth thee will not slumber.**
>
> —PSALM 121:1–3 (KJV)

After we determined that I probably didn't have any broken bones, I rolled over onto my knees and holding on to the boulders, stood up. Frank went to the Pond and came back with paper towels he had soaked with ice-cold water. He placed them on the scrapes on my head and knuckles. I knew God had been with me in preventing serious or fatal injury.

We decided that Wildcat Mountain would have to wait. Since we were in the middle of nowhere, I knew that, if at all possible, I would need to walk back to the start of the trail. I drank some water and took some deep breaths. My aluminum walking stick was bent. Frank straightened it and gave me one of his undamaged ones.

At the location where I fell, it would have been impossible for an ambulance or helicopter to rescue me. With God's help, I walked back the way we came—over and around dozens of rocks and boulders

We watched for signs of a concussion, and, except for a slight headache, there were none. I did not even need to seek an evaluation at the emergency room.

Early the next morning, we decided since it was the last full day of our vacation and I didn't have any major side effects from the previous day's fall, we would hike to Glen Ellis and Sabbaday Falls. They were well worth the effort. Both the trails in that area were well-maintained with few rocks and roots. On the elevations, they even had steps and handrails. Giant waterfalls thundered down to the river below in an awesome display of God's power.

Am I willing to try the Wildcat Mountain Trail again sometime? *No!* After the incident, I read the reviews of this trail and found out that experienced hikers classify it as "difficult and strenuous, and in some cases you may need spikes and climbing gear."

I've decided to stick with trails that are for beginner or moderate hikers. Also, I will remember that it would be extra prudent to read the reviews prior to tackling unfamiliar trails.

My miraculous fall at Wildcat Mountain reminds me that God is in control of my life, watching over me at all times.

God in the Midst of Trouble

By Janet Morris Grimes

On a whim, I decided I'd travel to an unfamiliar side of town to hear a guest speaker at a small church. Since autumn was teetering toward winter and darkness fell too early, I almost talked myself into wrapping up in a blanket on the sofa to sip a soothing cup of hot chocolate instead. But ultimately, I forced myself to follow the commands of my confusing GPS system to find this place I'd never been before.

Surprisingly, I ended up on a dead-end street. The church rose triumphantly in the distance, but getting to it from there would require that I drive through numerous yards to reach my destination. Not a good idea.

I turned around and finally found the church parking lot. As I put the car into park, I noticed I was running low on fuel. No matter. I'd take care of it later. I scurried inside and grabbed a seat in the back row, rattled, but present in the audience.

I jotted down many notes as the speaker told the group of ladies to take the hard path and never give up on whatever God had called them to do. Based on the Twenty-Third Psalm, the speaker touched on God's promise of an abundant life and the protection He provides:

You anoint my head with oil; my cup runs over. Surely goodness and mercy shall follow me all the days of my life; and I will dwell in the house of the LORD forever.

—Psalm 23:5–6 (NKJV)

Closing my notebook, I thanked God for the reminder. He keeps His word, always, and that particular scripture was printed on a laminated bookmark in my Bible.

My cup runs over.

I repeated this line with satisfaction as I strode to the car. I was thankful for the evening and ready to be back home with that blanket and hot chocolate. I stopped at the first gas station I could find. It was not in the best part of town, but I at least knew how to get home from that point.

Out of the corner of my eye, I saw someone in the shadows past the well-lit bay of gas pumps. My car was the only one parked there as I placed the pump in my tank.

A brisk wind blew through, and I zipped up my jacket.

I checked the pump again, locked my car, and ran inside the station to get a cup of hot chocolate for the ride home. I assumed the gas pump would shut itself off when the tank was full, like it always did.

Inside the store, I chose my beverage and was pressing the lid on my cup when someone said, "Ma'am, gas is pouring out of your car."

I turned to look into the eyes of a young man who used to be in our youth group at church. Though he was now an adult, in my eyes he'd always be a shy little boy, struggling to pronounce his *R*s and having the time of his life at church camp.

"Grant? Is that you?"

He nodded.

"Watch my cup. I'll be right back."

I rushed outside to turn off the pump. Gas was indeed over-flowing from my tank, puddling beneath my car.

I flipped off the switch, grabbed my receipt, and wiped the gas off my car with a few paper towels from a window cleaner bin. I hung my head as I went to the checkout counter to confess what I had done. The clerk slammed her hand against the counter.

"Great. Watch the store. I've got to get some sand."

I felt bad. It had been my mistake, but she wouldn't let me help.

I turned my attention back to Grant, who was still watching my hot chocolate. I hadn't seen him for a long time and had heard he'd gotten into some trouble.

I touched him on the shoulder. "Thanks for watching out for me. That was a stupid move. I should know better. Are you hungry?"

> "For my thoughts are not your thoughts, neither are your ways my ways," declares the LORD.
>
> —ISAIAH 55:8 (NIV)

His mouth twisted, so I started handing him things. A banana, a premade sandwich, a box of snack cakes, a container of milk…anything I could find within reach.

He broke into a smile while we watched the store together. I asked too many questions, yet he didn't ask me to stop, so we filled the next twenty minutes discussing old times, until the clerk returned. By this point, we all smelled like gasoline. Grant and I left while the clerk grabbed the phone to notify her supervisor.

"It's cold out here. Do you need a ride?" I asked.

He thought for a minute. "Sure. Thanks."

I had to crack the windows in the car for us to breathe while he told me about his legal troubles. He talked about how hard it was to be out on his own. "I've made some huge mistakes, but I think I'm going to turn myself in to get this behind me."

"That sounds good, Grant. There are consequences, but God still has a plan for you."

He nodded and gave me directions to his friend's house. Turn by turn, he clenched the bag of groceries in his lap.

"Will you be safe here, where I'm taking you?"

"Yes ma'am."

There they were. Those great manners I remembered. His precious grandmother had taught him well.

> **Therefore I glory in Christ Jesus in my service to God.**
>
> **—ROMANS 15:17 (NIV)**

He got out of the car and waved. His eyes seemed brighter, and my heart felt lighter.

"I'll be praying for you, Grant. Let me know how things turn out."

"Yes ma'am."

I pulled away and marveled at all the missteps that brought me to that gas station at that exact time and place. I knew my encounter with Grant was a divine appointment, and I was so thankful God brought us together, even as foolish as I felt for leaving the gas pump unattended.

I recalled again the Twenty-Third Psalm: "He restores my soul; he leads me in the paths of righteousness for His name's sake" (Psalm 23:3, NKJV).

For His name's sake?

GOD'S GIFT OF SMELL
— By Lawrence W. Wilson —

NASTY SMELLS CAN trigger the gag reflex—or even retching. That's not simply because they're unpleasant. God designed the human brain to interpret foul odor as a danger signal. That explains why people instinctively recoil at the smell of sour milk. Some animals have a more acute sense of smell, though their brains interpret scents differently. A dog may detect the scent of deadly diseases like cancer, yet will eat grass or dirt. Canines' idea of a foul odor is different because their bodies have different needs.

I chuckled as I realized even an unattended gas pump could be used to glorify God in some way.

Grant is now serving a sentence in a state prison. We've stayed in touch, and I still fully believe God has a plan for him.

That encounter left a lasting impression on me, but I didn't realize until much later the full scope of what had taken place.

When I was talking to Grant's grandmother at church about how Grant and I had bonded on that crazy night, I asked how he was doing. She grabbed my hand and said tearfully, "Honey, do you realize Grant was looking for someone to rob that night?"

I gulped. Not once did that ever cross my mind. Not once had I felt in danger as I invited him into my car.

All I knew is that on a lonely weeknight in the darkness, God used both of us to help each other, and maybe even prevent someone else from becoming a victim. I was amazed to become part of His story.

I shall merely try to help God as best I can, and if I succeed in doing that, then I shall be of use to others as well.

—Etty Hillesum, writer

CHAPTER 2

Meeting God through Helping Others

Miracles amid the Rubble

By Alice Klies

My stomach churned as I stood at what had been the entrance to my daughter's home…before a devastating tornado had ripped through Fort Worth.

A house once stood in this spot? Rubble of brick and wood lay scattered in front of me. Even the sod in the front lawn had been peeled away clean. I shook my head. *How did they possibly survive this?*

My daughter, Stacy, pointed to the only wall standing.

"We huddled there," she explained. "The noise roared around us. Our ears popped and the hair on our arms stood straight up from static electricity in the air."

She pointed to a beam that had speared the wall just above where she and her husband had shielded their three children with a mattress.

"I can't believe it, Mom. The kids screamed and cried, but I just felt calm. You know how I've felt Grandma around me all the time since she died? I heard her telling me everything would be all right."

Days later, we sifted through piles of bricks, plaster, glass, and insulation for salvageable items. As we sorted through belongings, I noted the miracle of God's grace. We found unbroken angels my daughter had collected throughout her life. Pictures of angels still attached to detached pieces of the wall stood out like beacons of light. We washed the ceramic angels that plaster and mud had battered. Once clean, they actually looked newer. Finding the angels suggested a brighter future. One after another, the angels showed up, and sifting through the rubble became almost fun. We started to laugh. I think God laughed right along with us because He can heal with laughter.

Stacy's neighbor visited us with her own amazing story. Just before the storm hit, she told her husband she needed to go to the store to get some mascara. He asked her not to go because the sky had turned gray and the stillness was so eerie. He knew they needed to shelter. Their home was barely damaged, and when she opened the front door after the storm, she looked down at the sidewalk to see an unopened package of mascara at her feet. Yep, God must have smiled.

> **He performs wonders that cannot be fathomed, miracles that cannot be counted.**
>
> —JOB 5:9 (NIV)

My grandchildren told me their own stories. "Grandma, my glasses were torn off my face, and the hair on my arms stood straight up. It was really scary."

"My body felt prickly all over, Grandma, and it was so loud I could hardly hear Mommy telling us we would be OK. I thought we were going to die!"

Carefully walking through the debris, we started to find irreplaceable photo albums and scrapbooks, just a little damp from the rain—memories saved that our family would cherish. As we searched, we kept commenting, "Things—just things—are gone, and yet look at us on our hands and knees. We are alive."

After this tornado experience, I was amazed to see help come from so many sources. The children's school collected money and furnished backpacks, uniforms, and school supplies for tornado victims. The Red Cross delivered boxes of clothing, shoes, and food staples. Friends, family, and total strangers showed up to dig through the remains and offer support. God heals fears, desperation, and sadness by giving us all of these human angels.

A relative purchased a better home for Stacy's family to rent—the kids made friends quickly, it was easier to get to their school, and my daughter had a shorter commute to work.

The outpouring of love from so many strangers affected Stacy. Her compassion for others grew. My grandchildren also learned a lot about giving. When news stories told of disasters in their city, my grandchildren became the first ones to ask, "Can we help?"

Amid the rubble and in Stacy's presence, I knew I was seeing miracles. I believe God's healing ability and grace show up when we least expect it. When life becomes difficult, we can feel His continual presence in unexpected ways.

I believe God let me be a part of this experience and outcome with my daughter to remind me that He is in control. If I trust Him, He will deliver some good out of something bad, although not always the way I expect—maybe by leaving just a few unbroken angels to share His promise of hope to those of us tramping through the rubble or by letting one of His daughters feel her grandmother's presence from heaven.

When God Has
Other Plans

By Adriana Vaughn

David's eyes twinkled at me as we pinched off pieces of the squishy Ethiopian bread called injera to scoop up hummus. I doubted he would be someone I would spend my life with, but my friend Tambra had convinced me to go on this third date.

"Did I mention I took ballet folklórico in high school?"

David grinned, probably hoping my heart would pitter-patter. How did this man know so much about my Hispanic culture? He wore a blue plaid shirt and lounged on the couch opposite me. I studied every feature: the red-tinged curly hair, the fluffy beard I'd like to trim, and the strong hands that revealed his heart for the outdoors. Surrounded in the aroma of ginger, curry, and basil, we giggled and swapped stories about teaching English.

When the waiter brought the bill, David grabbed it and said, "Would you be offended if I use a coupon?"

I quickly reassured him that was OK, but I held back on stating that frugality is my love language.

The next morning, with my beagle lying next to me so that one of his ears flopped over the right side of my journal, I wrote, "Is this guy the one?"

I was prepared to go back overseas to continue language study and teach refugees, but I also wanted to be married before

I turned forty. Then I remembered the verse from Hebrews God had spoken to my heart before I moved to the Middle East.

Three years earlier, my former college roommate, who then lived in Central Asia, came to my hometown, Houston, for a visit, and we had gone shopping together. While I had been teaching public school in Texas for the past decade, Marie had spent the last ten years living abroad. She chattered to me as if the clock were ticking, and she needed to talk fast enough to get all her words out.

> **And we know that in all things God works for the good of those who love him, who have been called according to his purpose.**
>
> **—ROMANS 8:28 (NIV)**

"Guess who I ran into? Bill, the director of the language institute where I taught. He's recruiting Christians willing to work in the Middle East." She paused and eyed me. "I've been praying, and I think that group is for you."

Goose bumps erupted all over my body. I couldn't look at her. I'd always wanted to teach in another country, but I'd never envisioned living in the Middle East.

Me, go overseas? Nope. I'm a single, thirty-five-year-old woman, and moving to a place with fewer prospects for a husband doesn't sound appealing.

"Umm. I'll pray about it," I said to her.

I didn't.

A few weeks later, I met with Jaime, my friend since college. I sat inside the Mediterranean restaurant waiting for her. A woman with a cute pink hat entered. I recognized her walk and the light-up-the-room smile, but this woman had no hair. I stood up to call her over.

"Jaime."

She drew me into a hug. "I guess I should've told you I lost my hair."

After we ordered, Jamie admitted she didn't have much of an appetite anymore, and asked, "So, what's up with you?"

Here was a brave woman receiving cancer treatment, asking about my life.

"I think I'm supposed to go overseas, but I'm afraid I'll stay single for the rest of my life."

Jaime stared at me, her mouth slightly open and a glint in her eyes, "You know, I finally married my high school sweetheart. We moved to China. We fulfilled my longing for adoption, and then I got pregnant. It seemed like all my dreams had come true, and then I got cancer, a diagnosis I didn't want. This isn't the life I chose, but I had to come to a point of surrender and choose to trust God. Adriana, I think you need to obey God, go overseas, and surrender to God your desire to be married."

> But seek first the kingdom of God and his righteousness, and all these things will be added to you.
>
> —MATTHEW 6:33 (ESV)

I stopped breathing for a moment. I couldn't seem to taste the hummus on the bread, although I noticed Jaime had found her appetite and managed to devour her entire sandwich and fries. I nodded. What do you say to a woman's wisdom when she's in the fight for her life?

That Sunday morning, I headed to church and sat in the third row, alone like every other Sunday. During worship, one of the pastors announced, "I feel like God is issuing new assignments this morning. If that's you, come to the altar."

I felt as if the pastor was speaking to me, but I didn't want to go overseas and face being single forever.

No one in the congregation responded. After what I thought was an eternity, I drifted past three rows to the altar where I dropped to my knees. I closed my eyes. *God, I surrender.*

Immediately, a verse popped in my head. I scurried back to my seat and opened my Bible to Hebrews 10:35–37 (NIV): "So do not throw away your confidence; it will be richly rewarded. You need to persevere so that when you have done the will of God, you will receive what he has promised. For, 'In just a little while, he who is coming will come and will not delay.'"

The last verse quotes the exact same verse from Habakkuk 2 that I had written across the long list of attributes of the husband I had been praying for over the past year. Was God promising me a husband after I obeyed?

Although I didn't join the group my friend had suggested, two years later, my teaching experience opened a door to teach intensive English at a university in Kuwait. To get away from the desert during the Christmas season, I visited my former college roommate, Marie, who now lived in a country along the Mediterranean. She took me to a Christmas Eve service at her church. I wandered into a large room with metal chairs. The congregation of expatriates from around the world sang familiar Christmas songs in English.

A middle-aged woman wearing a leather jacket over a sweater marched to the front. I learned she was the pastor's wife. "I feel like I'm supposed to talk about God's promises today." She opened her Bible.

"Do not throw away your confidence…" The pastor's wife kept reading through the next verse, the same passage that the Holy Spirit brought to my mind that morning at the altar a couple of years earlier.

I closed my eyes as tears poured down my cheeks. *God, You haven't forgotten me.*

Almost a year after I visited Marie, I returned to teach a second year in Kuwait, but this time my loneliness intensified. My roommate had returned home to the United States, my Syrian neighbors had moved out, my language tutor had relocated, and even my coworker and his family had moved to the other side of town. I tried to hang a few wall decorations, so the space would feel less empty. But one of the decorations, the image of a tree I wanted to put on the wall to add some life, just wouldn't stick. I tried to press the adhesive down more, but no luck. I gave up on it and the tears slid down my cheeks.

God, why can't I have a husband? No one is here to help. No one is here to tell me if this decoration is crooked or not. I grabbed my Bible study book to encourage myself. Sitting on the couch, I opened the book to the first section. The focus verse was Hebrews 10:35—the same verse from last year's Christmas service that the pastor's wife had shared. I crouched over the book, holding my face in my hands, sobbing. *God, how much longer?*

Now, a year later, back home in Houston after that third date with David, I wondered if I should keep dating him. With my beagle at my heels, I located the Bible I'd used before moving overseas. I turned to Hebrews 10:35–37. In the right margin of my Bible, I saw my note: "10/16/2011 God promises a mate." I had just learned that David's birthday was October 16.

GOD'S GIFT OF TASTE
— By Lawrence W. Wilson —

BABIES ARE BORN with a dislike for bitter tastes. Yet some kids go on to love lemon drops while others turn up their nose at any green vegetable. While we all have individual tastes, research shows that the difference between the two is largely due to exposure. Children who are introduced to a variety of foods before age two are likely to develop an expansive diet. The good news here is that there is hope for adults with a narrow palate. By sampling different foods, it is possible to acquire an appreciation for new flavors.

We married the next summer just six months before my fortieth birthday.

By giving me a husband, God ended my loneliness and shame of not having a permanent date. Through the repetition of the Hebrews verses, He showed me that He was my constant companion and fully aware of my needs and desires.

In that season of being single yet longing to be married, I learned God shows Himself through friends, leaders, and even in books. Still, He didn't just let me sit around to mope over what I didn't have. Instead, God invited me into the adventure of following Him, and then grew in me what I needed—a heart to persevere beyond what I thought possible. His continual presence enabled me to endure and thrive.

Heart's Desire

By Elizabeth W. Peterson

I still remember the smell of cedar from the chest I used to prop up a chalkboard taller than I was. I turned it sideways so I could write alphabet letters, spelling, and math for my dolls and stuffed animals that I lined up to face me, their preschool teacher. I called the roll, raised up Sally's plastic doll hand for her to answer "Here," and started my lesson. My child-sized fingers moved Ted's brown furry legs up to the chalkboard to write his alphabet letters.

When I turned twenty-one, my desire to become a teacher became reality. I was in an actual classroom filled with high school students who, unlike my childhood dolls and stuffed animals, were not always eager to learn. But I was up for the challenge.

I never imagined doing anything other than teaching until my right hand became too weak to write on the board. The changes happened so gradually that I hardly noticed them. After I wrote only a few lines on the board, my right arm grew too heavy to write. *No problem,* I thought. *Students are always eager to write on the board.*

But the solution was not so simple on days when my right leg dragged as I carried loads of books and papers to my car to look over before the next day. An hour's nap on the couch restored my energy enough to wipe away traces of worry.

Still, I wondered why my legs could not make it up the steps without my resting or why I couldn't get back down without holding tightly to the rail.

Determined to keep pressing on in my classroom, I modified daily routines. I spent more time sitting at my desk and less time walking down rows of desks to assist students. Then one day I collapsed in the classroom beside an alarmed student. The school nurse came running, and after that event I knew that it was time to seek medical advice.

> **Delight yourself also in the LORD, and He shall give you the desires of your heart.**
>
> **—PSALM 37:4 (NKJV)**

I watched the neurologist's rubber hammer tap up and down my arms and legs, checking reflexes. "Looks OK," he said, "but let's get an MRI just to be sure."

His answer to questions about my difficulty writing on the board was "teacher shoulder." He patted my arm and laughed as he said he was married to a teacher and gave me an all-knowing look.

A few days later the neurologist called with the results of my MRI. "Well, the tests show that plaque has developed along the myelin sheath and are shorting out signals that are needed to make your arms and legs move." He went on to say that because of this, I could have multiple sclerosis, but more tests would have to be run to rule out other causes.

Multiple sclerosis? Nerve signals shorting out? Signals that move my arms and legs? *Too much information,* I thought. Didn't doctors call you into their office and reveal such news slowly to a patient? Or was I thinking only of what they did in TV dramas?

I tried to process all this and heard myself ask, "Will I still be able to teach?"

"No reason why you shouldn't," he said. "Come back in six months for a follow-up and we'll talk."

"No, Lord," I cried as I placed the phone down. I thought of a lovely lady in our church who lived with MS with genuine difficulty.

Several months after Susan had first been diagnosed with MS, we watched her struggle to walk—first with a cane, then a walker. Gradually she retreated to her home and finally, to a nursing home. She became only a name on the church prayer list.

> **May He grant you according to your heart's desire, and fulfill all your purpose.**
>
> **—PSALM 20:4 (NKJV)**

I remember before Susan was diagnosed how she had always walked briskly down church halls to serve wherever she was needed, That memory of her abilities suddenly swept away by a chronic disease brought questions. Was this God's time for her and for me to experience a debilitating disease? Would God allow me time to teach the next five years and then retire?

Family and friends prayed for remission, but the weakness in my right arm and leg increased. Like my friend Susan, I soon needed a cane to maintain my balance and hobble down school hallways that seemed to grow longer as my steps became slower.

Sadness filled the averted eyes of teachers who had taught with me for more than twenty years as I passed by them in the hall.

Don't they notice my attractive canes, I thought, as I mustered up the strength to say hello and smile.

The time came too soon when the cane no longer supported my weakening body, and reluctantly I exchanged the cane for a walker. Outwardly I boasted of how I could carry books in the basket of what one friend called my four-by-four that I bravely pushed to my classroom. Inside, I grieved the loss of the mobility I had once enjoyed.

Too soon, four years later, I needed a power chair to navigate the long hall. I could sit at a teaching station designed to help me function in the classroom, but other barriers emerged. Getting in and out of the car and into the school safely brought new concerns. My husband began to take me to school and pick me up, but this made him lose work time. We considered adapting the van with hand controls, but we still wondered if I'd have strength to endure an eight-hour day at school.

Was God telling me it was time for me to leave the job I loved? He had given me wisdom to choose the right therapies and adaptations to continue to teach. Now, was He leading me to leave?

I put my name on everybody's prayer list, requesting that they ask God to strengthen me so that I could teach one more year. I knew that God could fully restore my feeble body and was ready for Him to bring even partial restoration.

In spite of friends' petitions for God to heal my body, over the next few months I showed signs of losing more mobility.

The day I had to write a resignation letter to the principal came sooner than I had wanted. With much sadness I said farewell to faculty who understood my grief. With only the best intentions, they asked me what I would do with my time after I left.

"There is life after teaching," I said, trying to disguise hints of sorrow. But to close friends, I could not hide my grief.

"Teaching is my whole identity," I told them. "I feel I have lost who I am." They could only nod.

"What will I do if I can no longer teach?" I sobbed to a close friend.

"You can start meeting me here in the church prayer garden to pray," she said.

Our prayer time became something I looked forward to each week. We met to pray for the needs of church members. My request was only one item on long lists.

At first praying seemed to be an insignificant job, but it became a major part of my life. Praying for others enabled me to take the focus off myself and put it on God. As I allowed God to teach me, I became His student.

In God's classroom I learned to do what I had always demanded that my students do: listen to instruction. During those days with His teaching, God began to direct me to where He wanted me to be—not where my heart wanted to go. Proverbs 16:9 (NKJV) tells us, "A man's heart plans his way, but the LORD directs his steps."

God's timing and directing became clear to me when a mother in our church phoned me, asking if I could teach her child in my home. I had never considered the possibility of parents bringing their children to me, but God surely had.

Teaching in my home opened a new world for me. Flashcards with magnets soon lined my refrigerator. Colorful tags of words taped to objects resembled the classroom where I had once taught a roomful of students.

Seated in my wheelchair at my dining room table, I taught homeschoolers. Using online tutoring platforms, I added students who lived in all four time zones.

GOD'S GIFT OF SIGHT
— By Tez Brooks —

IN 2 KINGS 6:15–17 (NIV), a servant boy saw an enemy army surrounding the city. Running to his master Elisha, he asked, "What shall we do?" Elisha told him not to fear: "Those who are with us are more than those who are with them." Elisha asked God to open the boy's eyes to see the mountain was full of horses and chariots of fire. Immediately, the servant saw the hosts of heaven standing ready to fight for them. What a gift— to perceive the protection of God. Christians can't always see God at work during a crisis, but He is always there.

And God's grace did not end there. Such amazing privileges give new meaning to Paul's words to the Corinthian believers and to me: "And God is able to make all grace abound toward you, that you, always having all sufficiency in all things, may have an abundance for every good work" (2 Corinthians 9:8, NKJV).

God had a plan for my life when as a child I was seated on the floor with my imaginary students. His grace abounded while the rage of disease threatened to end what I held dear in life. God poured out blessings and placed me in exactly the right classroom with exactly the right students so that I might abound in continuing to do the job I loved. He never left me or forsook me.

God's Seat Assignment

By Cindy Shufflebarger

I despised assigned seats in school as a child and even more so as a teenager. I was much more interested in having fun than in doing work. Assigned seats usually removed my distractions and left me more likely to focus on the task at hand—the work of learning.

Not much has changed since I have become an adult. I still prefer the freedom to choose my seat. Whether it's on an airplane, at a sporting event, or at the theater, I want to make the choice. However, sometimes I choose poorly. Maybe I didn't know the venue and selected a seat with a poor view. Or I picked seats not knowing that a 6-foot-5-inch person would be sitting in front of my petite self—leaving me with a perfect view of the back of his head for the evening.

Other times, it's just not possible to choose and seats are randomly assigned. A recent experience on a trip to visit my daughter reminded me that our seat assignment is sometimes beyond our control, but in God's perspective, can be better than we expected.

Excited to visit my daughter, I arrived at the airport early. I was flying to her college town to spend the weekend with her. As I walked to the gate, I noticed an earlier flight was departing for the same destination at one gate before my assigned one. An agent was still at the gate, but the flight was scheduled to depart in less than five minutes and all passengers had already boarded.

I briefly pondered if it was worth my time to even ask about the possibility of switching to the earlier flight. My recent experiences told me that surely the flight would be full, there would be an exorbitant fee to make the change, or, in the slim chance that they had space, they would not want to prolong the boarding with an additional passenger.

As I started to walk by, the agent looked up and made eye contact. I smiled. He smiled in return, so I approached the counter and hesitantly asked if I could board this plane instead of my later flight. Much to my surprise, he reported that there was an available seat and he would happily switch me to this flight without any fees.

> **Many are the plans in the mind of a man, but it is the purpose of the Lord that will stand.**
>
> —PROVERBS 19:21 (ESV)

I practically sprinted down the jetway to board the plane before anyone could decide there had been a mistake. Surely this good fortune was a gift, and I uttered a prayer of thanksgiving.

As I made my way to the back of the plane, it became clear there was only one row remaining that had an unoccupied seat. As most of the overhead bin compartments had already been filled and secured, I took the first available space and clumsily hoisted my bag in the air and wrangled it into the narrow space. I continued down the aisle as people stared. I was clearly a latecomer.

Nearing my seat, I saw the young woman I'd be sitting next to was in some sort of distress. Crying, with panic written on her face, she was frantically talking to someone on her cell phone. I smiled sympathetically as I settled in my seat and whispered a prayer asking God to help me in the uncertainty of the situation.

I'm not great at small talk. I'm also not great at ignoring someone in pain. And so, I leaned in gently and asked if she was OK, followed by the slightly riskier question inquiring if she needed anything. She quickly shared that she wrestled with anxiety, was terrified of flying, and that she was flying across the country to see her dying father. Her boss had gifted her the plane ticket and the time off from work. Now she faced three dreadful flights before arriving at her destination, where she'd face the emotional stress of saying goodbye to her father.

> I am the vine; you are the branches. Whoever abides in me and I in him, he it is that bears much fruit, for apart from me you can do nothing.
>
> —JOHN 15:5 (ESV)

I gently nodded as I slowly inhaled, then exhaled, thinking that God had placed me here for a reason. My eyes were doing most of the talking because a mask covered my face due to COVID-19 restrictions.

Not really knowing anything about her, I asked if I could pray with her. A look of gratitude washed over her as she accepted, while telling me that her grandmother used to pray with her as a child.

I instinctively reached for her hand despite COVID-19 cautions, while wondering if she'd be offended by my gesture.

As I held her hand and prayed, she relaxed. Her entire demeanor changed with the touch of my hand and the short prayer muffled through a mask. Her respiration rate returned to normal, and we made friendly conversation for a few more minutes while the flight attendants scurried about making final preparations.

Soon it was time for takeoff, and her anxiety escalated beyond anything I had seen. Again, I held her hand, talked calmly, walked her through some visual imagery, and did anything I could think of to distract her from the sounds and sensations of taking flight. Once in the air, she slowly recovered, and we continued to chat for a few minutes. At one point, she offered me the other half of the sandwich she was carrying with her. I graciously declined but chuckled to myself—clearly she wasn't bothered by me holding her hand during a pandemic if she was offering to share her food with me.

Time ticked on slowly as I sat in awkwardness, trying to determine if I should continue conversation with her, or if I should I give her some space. She soon discovered the entertainment system on the seat back in front of her and was amused in childlike fashion. I was pleased that she was no longer consumed with her fear of flying. She even had moments of enjoying the beautiful views outside the window. At one point, she took a selfie with me, indicating that she wanted to remember my kindness.

As the landing approached, her anxiety ramped up again. I repeated the strategies that had soothed her during takeoff and commended her for her bravery. I reminded her to think of this flight's success as she boarded her next flight. She repeatedly expressed gratitude and jokingly asked if I would come with her on her remaining two flights. She said she was praying that she'd have someone like me seated next to her again. I prayed with her, and we parted ways.

GOD'S GIFT OF TOUCH
— By Lawrence W. Wilson —

NERVE FIBERS IN the skin have specialized, corpuscular ends that can register touch, pain, temperature, itch, and other sensations. Many of these receptors are concentrated in the hands. Recent scientific research has revealed that the sense of touch in the fingertips is so sophisticated that it can detect the difference between two surfaces that differ only in the topmost layer of molecules. That difference in texture is undetectable by the human eye. No wonder the word *touchy* has come to mean highly sensitive in terms of emotions. Human touch can register information that cannot be detected by any other sense, even the eye.

I continued to pray for her during the week that followed, but I have no idea how things went with her father or where she is now. Nonetheless, I'm grateful that God orchestrated a change in my travel plans that day.

While I may never fully know the outcome of my encounter with her, I'm glad that I said yes to the prompting of the Holy Spirit to reach out and pray with her. Perhaps she's already forgotten our exchange. But I haven't. It continues to remind me that God is gracious, He provides, and He arranges divine appointments. He chose my seat that day and allowed me to encourage this woman whom I might not have met otherwise. He is always present and at work, and He invites us to join Him in what He's doing around us.

The Christmas Miracle

By Dianne Fraser

For several years, I had the privilege of coordinating the Angel Tree project in my area. Angel Tree is a ministry of Prison Fellowship, through which people provide Christmas gifts for children on behalf of their incarcerated parent. These children are the unspoken victims of crime; they suffer the consequences of their parent's mistakes. They don't only miss having a parent at home, but they also miss out on little joyful experiences— like receiving a Christmas gift from their mom or dad. People who participate in the Angel Tree program have a beautiful opportunity to live out compassionately the very heart of Jesus. He told us that what we do for others, we do for him: "I was in prison and you came to visit me" (Matthew 25:36, NIV).

One particular year, I had a long list of people who had applied for Angel Tree gifts for the coming Christmas. Around eighty children from twenty-five families had been identified and nominated—but since we had only a congregation of 250 in our small Australian town, it was a huge ask. So, I sat in my home office, wondering where to start.

I began the process of contacting the children's caregivers, seeking insight into whether a gift would be welcome, and if so, what might be a meaningful present from the parent. As I made my way through the list, many stories pulled at my heartstrings: The single mother with two severely disabled children, left to parent alone while her husband served time. The grandparents whose granddaughter lived with them, since both parents were imprisoned. The older sister, caring for her young brother, who told me they had kept the matter quiet to everyone around them since her brother felt so ashamed of his imprisoned parents. So many situations that I could hardly imagine having to live with. Feelings of helplessness washed over me time and again. Phone call after phone call, the task was getting bigger. The many stories of the children and caregivers were unbearably heartbreaking, and I soon realized I couldn't trim the project down in any way.

> **He has sent me to bind up the brokenhearted, to proclaim freedom for the captives and release from darkness for the prisoners.**
>
> **—ISAIAH 61:1 (NIV)**

I set up a time to present the matter to the church on a Sunday morning. I felt God telling me to share the stories of these families and let Him do the rest.

And so I did. When I had finished, there was barely a dry eye in the house (including my own), and the rush to partner with me was profound. God awakened our church family to the love we needed to share. Not only did we have enough pledges to purchase presents for the eighty children, but twenty-five caregivers would also receive gifts—and a food hamper for each affected family as well! So many people told me how participating in the event rebirthed a sense of purpose in their own lives.

In the process of contacting and connecting with individuals and families, I was especially drawn to Ella. Ella was a grandmother who cared for her fifteen-year-old granddaughter, Zoe. Both of Zoe's parents were in jail, and this was their second stint inside. Ella's quiet grace and confidence drew me in. She was unassuming, gentle, and grateful. She welcomed the idea of the gifts and suggested a few items that Zoe might appreciate. I decided I would be responsible for this family.

> **If you spend yourselves in behalf of the hungry and satisfy the needs of the oppressed, then your light will rise in the darkness, and your night will become like the noonday.**
>
> **—ISAIAH 58:10 (NIV)**

As I shopped, I asked God to show me the perfect gifts. A bottle of nail polish, hair accessories, and some adorable fluffy pink socks with a matching beanie found their way into my shopping cart. As I wrapped the presents, I prayed for the family. As I wrote out the card and penciled their names, I asked God to work a miracle in their lives.

The first in-person encounter was at the pickup point for the gifts. I was delighted to meet Zoe and Ella. As I handed Zoe the gifts and told her they were from her mom and dad, she cried. She went and sat in their car and looked at the card while I chatted with Ella.

I handed Ella a gift too.

"What's this for?" she asked.

"It's for you."

"I'm confused; I thought this was for the kids."

"It is, but our church community wants to bless you too. You are doing a wonderful job with Zoe, and we want to celebrate you and tell you that we are here for you. We also want to tell you that God loves you and sees you as well."

That sent her off in a torrent of tears. Hardly able to speak, she just whispered, "Thank you."

As she calmed, she was able to share that it would be the first Christmas gift she had had for years—there was nobody to bless her that way. That broke my heart.

After navigating through that, I then pulled a hamper from the back seat of my car. The hamper had all the traditional treats of Christmas, from crackers and crisps to juices and chocolates. There were gift vouchers for the bakery, the butcher, and the supermarket. Enough for a complete Christmas experience. Ella's tears began to roll again.

Finally, I handed her the fuel card that one member of our congregation had purchased to include in the hampers. Enough for a full tank. At that, she fell to her knees and sobbed.

Zoe stepped out of the car in concern and hugged her grandmother. I filled her in on what the gifts were, and Zoe explained.

"We weren't able to travel to see Mum and Dad for Christmas as Gran can't afford the cost to get there. You have just made it so I can see them on Christmas Day."

By this stage, all three of us were hugging and crying—enjoying a moment of celebration in the midst of a broken situation.

I thought that was the end of this story, but it wasn't. We forget God is often at work with a parallel story, and so it was in this case. The other side of this story was unfolding in prison.

Zoe's mother was wrestling with her situation and the guilt of not being present for her teenage daughter. The chaplains were speaking deep truths into her life, and a desperate desire for change and transformation was being born. When the idea of Angel Tree was presented, she was quick to apply and hoped she'd be able to take part.

Zoe's mother shared with the chaplains that she was battling at several levels. How could God forgive her? How could she believe that a God she had never given a moment of thought to over her life would be interested in her? Upon her release, how would she survive in the outside world and find a better community where she could make good choices? How could she provide for her daughter when she felt hopeless in every area of her life? Deep and troubling questions tumbled around in her soul.

The concept of God's grace was unfathomable to her—and then a tangible example and experience of God's constant love for her arrived on Christmas Day.

As Zoe hugged her mother tight and Ella shared the story of the gifts, fuel card, and Christmas hamper, something was birthed in their journey to a better future.

Several weeks later, a letter arrived at the church, addressed to me. Inside was a letter from Zoe's mother.

Dear Dianne,

You don't know me, but you purchased a Christmas gift on my behalf for my daughter Zoe. I want to ask you to thank the people in your church for showing my family so much love and care. You don't even know us, and yet you were part of God changing my life forever.

The chaplain has helped me see that the care you showed with Angel Tree is just like God's love for me. That I don't deserve

it, but God loves me so much He sent you my way for me to
understand that me and my whole family matter and that He
forgives me for the bad things I have done.

Zoe's mother was released several months later and spent
her first weekend in a local church, being loved and restored.
Eventually Zoe came to Christ, and finally Ella, too, was rescued for eternity.

We don't know how often God uses a simple word, an
action, a message of hope to transform a life. We don't know
how frequently a prompting in our spirit is a direct message
from God—a call to act on His behalf. As Isaiah says, God
sends us into His work, and we are invited to be part of His
story in the lives of others. And just because we can't see it,
that doesn't mean it's not unfolding.

We are all wounded. But wounds are necessary for his healing light to enter into our beings. Without wounds and failures and frustrations and defeats, there will be no opening for his brilliance to trickle in and invade our lives.

—Bo Sanchez, author and minister

CHAPTER 3
God's Healing Touch

Saying "Yes!" to God

By Rose McCormick Brandon

When I sensed God calling me to open my home for a neighborhood Bible study, I shared the idea with a friend from church who lived nearby. She was eager to help, so the two of us, both stay-at-home moms, set out on this venture together.

For me, saying yes to the home study led to founding a local chapter of an international Christian women's organization. My work with the organization involved encouraging other women in our Canadian border city to open their homes for Bible study. Many were eager to host and to teach.

Soon, a network of women's Bible studies spread out over the city. Many of those who attended had never read the Bible, but they opened their hearts to the message of Jesus and invited Him in.

As a result of the studies, we started holding monthly evening meetings in a downtown hotel and designed them for people who did not know about or have a relationship with God. At each meeting one or two local women would tell how they came to know Jesus. Then a guest speaker would give a presentation and end the evening by inviting people to turn their lives over to Christ.

More women came to the Lord, and within a few months, new Bible studies started. God provided several experienced Bible teachers, and they were a special gift to the many new believers who were bringing their husbands and children to Christ. It was an exciting time: In every area of the ministry God supplied helpers while also supplying me with the energy, time, and passion I needed.

The international leaders of the women's organization encouraged people like me, who held leadership positions at the community level, to dedicate as much time to the churches we attended as we did to community ministry. Parachurch organizations, such as the one I was associated with, were attracting people from all denominations. Not every congregation was comfortable with the influx of excited believers that filled their pews. Attending regular services and dedicating time to the programs of our local churches seemed like a remedy for these concerns.

> **If you're serious about living this new resurrection life with Christ, *act* like it. Pursue the things over which Christ presides.**
>
> **—COLOSSIANS 3:1 (MSG)**

The time I spent on this women's ministry increased as the work grew. Family life became more complicated when my husband's job became more demanding and our children added sports, music, and other activities to their schedules. My goal had always been to put my husband and children first, which hadn't been a problem until I added church responsibilities like singing in the choir, teaching Sunday school, and various other jobs to my schedule.

For several years, I pursued excellence in all that I did, a recurring theme in books and sermons at the time. I assumed that excellence meant doing everything required of me, whether in church or community. If the pastor asked me to take on a church task, I never considered saying no. Sometimes it seemed that every minute of every day in my life was earmarked for something.

I enjoyed most of the responsibilities, but still, overcommitment began to get the best of me. I began to suffer from fatigue and migraines. When I was alone, which wasn't often, I would weep for no reason. The phone rang too often. My to-do list was too long. Too many people needed my attention. Sometimes it was a struggle just to be civil. I felt like a runner who had used up all her energy in the first few kilometers of the race and had no strength left to reach the finish line.

> **Listen when your father corrects you. Pay attention and learn good judgment, for I am giving you good guidance. Don't turn away from my instructions.**
>
> **—PROVERBS 4:1, 2 (NLT)**

Jesus said in Matthew 5:3 (MSG), "You're blessed when you're at the end of your rope. With less of you there is more of God and his rule." With my fingers barely clinging to the end of my rope, I was forced to ask myself, "What am I doing wrong?"

I had to admit that I was a people pleaser. What would the pastor and others think of me if I admitted I was exhausted and needed to quit my church activities? Conclusion: I cared too much about what they thought and not enough about what God thought.

I was depriving my family too. This became serious when I accepted a full-time job in our church. When I hadn't been working outside the home, I was able to spend quality time with my family. But this new job added a demanding dimension to my life, and it became impossible for me to divide my time between family, ministry, and church. There just wasn't enough of me to go around.

I was in a weak place—physically, emotionally, and spiritually. Several times I opened various books and devotionals and this verse appeared: "'Martha, Martha,' the Lord answered, 'you are worried and upset about many things'" (Luke 10:41, NIV). Though I knew God's presence was constantly with me, I could no longer feel Him because I had crowded Him out, along with other important people like my family. I could not continue down the Martha path. I had to make changes.

After much prayer, I came up with an idea that put me on the path to healing. I suggested to the church board that they hire a college student to take my place for the summer months. They agreed. My husband and I bought a trailer located in a park on a bay on Lake Huron, an hour's drive from home. Our family of five lived there for July and August. This revived my body and soul. We had no television and no activities to run to—just trips to the local country library and lots of boating, fishing, swimming, and campfires. My quiet times were never rushed. I often sat by the water and prayed. I could feel myself healing.

When fall came, I made another change. I stopped working on Mondays. That gave me a three-day weekend—an extra day to clean house, do the laundry, and catch up on household duties. I began to breathe normally again. But this wasn't the end of my healing journey.

I am an avid reader of Selwyn Hughes's devotionals, *Every Day with Jesus*. One day I read how Hughes, too, had suffered from the stresses of taking on too many obligations. He wrote, "I've learned to say no to many things in order to say yes to the main thing."

That sentence stuck in my mind. I needed to practice saying no. And I needed to practice saying it in church. Hughes's advice was simple and practical. Going in too many directions had made me ill. Healing would come from focusing on the main things God had in store for me. I finally recognized that what I had been taught about giving equal time to the local church and my calling to community ministry had no basis in Scripture. It was OK for me to say no, even in church.

As my commitments diminished, I began to feel like a new person. I went for walks and took time for simple things like gardening. Being outdoors and working with the soil and plants were healing for me too. There I became quiet enough to unburden my soul to the Lord and allow Him to guide me in the process of pruning excess from my life.

Another interesting thing happened. I ended up in the hospital and had surgery. Nothing life threatening, but serious enough that I had to rest for six weeks. Those healing weeks allowed me to think deeply about my future.

I continued to teach the Bible to women because this was a passion from the Lord. After much prayer and contemplation, I concluded that ministering through writing and teaching were the things I wanted to focus on, so I began to say no to most other requests. If the request was a one-time obligation and not an ongoing responsibility, like a speaking engagement, and if it didn't interfere with my family or the main things in my life, I gave myself permission to say yes.

GOD'S GIFT OF SIGHT

— By Lawrence W. Wilson —

IT IS SAID that a camera never lies because it simply records the light it absorbs. The eye, however, can be fooled. Or rather, the brain can. Photoreceptor cells in the eye turn light into energy, which is transmitted to the brain. The brain converts these impulses into the images we see. However, the brain then interprets the images to make sense of them. That's where the possibility of deception comes in. For example, the brain can draw the wrong conclusion by mistaking the insect *Phasmatodea* ("walking stick") for a twig. Seeing is often, but not always, believing.

Not long after my recovery from surgery, I resigned from my job at the church. The headaches subsided, and other signs of stress diminished.

Turns out that by saying no to others I was saying yes to the Lord and His healing touch.

A Change in Plans

By Caroline S. Cooper

"What do you want to be when you grow up?"

My hand rose quickly, and I practically bounced up and down in my seat. By fifth grade, I already knew my answer. I wanted to be a teacher of music, math, or English. I loved school, and those were my favorite classes. I believed God was preparing me for such a purpose. Even at this young age, I yearned to leave my childhood behind.

My shy smile hid a traumatic secret. I was the victim of childhood sexual abuse that impacted my ability to form healthy relationships. At school, my academic success coupled with my introverted personality and poor social skills resulted in me feeling that I did not fit in. Several of the "cool" boys in my class identified me as an easy target of teasing and called me unflattering nicknames. They probably had no idea how deeply it hurt. I had only a small circle of friends but did not socialize outside of school. I looked forward to a future that I hoped would relieve me of my pain.

"Where do you see yourself in five years? Ten years?"

I was in high school, and my youth group leader asked us to think about our future and write down our thoughts. What goals did we have? What possibilities did we see ahead? Graduation would be the beginning of a new adventure, and I welcomed the assignment.

My pen scrawled across the page as fast as my hand had risen years before. I had expanded my career goals to include an over-all life plan, including teaching in a small town where I would meet my future spouse and have our children—my ideal life.

It never crossed my mind that God would have other plans.

By the time I graduated from college, my life had departed significantly from my plan. I had married my college sweetheart before finishing school and moved six hundred miles away from home to a big city. I completed a music education degree, but we moved to the Kansas City area the summer I graduated and all potential teaching jobs were filled. A couple of years later, I decided

> We can make our plans, but the LORD determines our steps.
>
> —PROVERBS 16:9 (NLT)

to apply for a job as a band director, but discovered I was preg-nant with my first child and chose to stay home with my baby. My plan of teaching in a public school never came to pass.

God has a way of surprising us as life takes unexpected twists and turns. His timing causes events to take place at a pace that does not always match our preference. We can only navigate change with Him because His purpose takes priority over our plans. Job 42:1–2 (NLT) tells us, "Then Job replied to the LORD: 'I know that you can do anything, and no one can stop you.'"

One of the most dramatic detours in my life happened shortly after my fortieth birthday. An emotional breakdown brought me to my knees, and I cried out desperately to the Lord. In grace and mercy, God responded to my prayers and those of many others. God healed me of the post-traumatic stress disorder (PTSD) that lay buried in my soul due to the childhood sexual abuse. Ignoring the problem had not made it go away. God used a ten-day program at a psychiatric hospital to start me down a path to healing. I began intensive therapy to treat clinical depression and anxiety, and a friend at church invited me to participate in a Christian twelve-step group. During this time my family gave unconditional love and support even as they struggled beside me.

The journey of recovery took me through the highs of success and the lows of setbacks. But God was a constant presence, preparing and equipping me to serve Him in a way I never expected.

"What do you want to be when you grow up?"

Serving as the leader of a mental health support group would not have made it on my list. But by the time I passed my forty-fifth birthday, God had revealed that He desired me to serve Him by supporting others who encountered challenges similar to what I had faced.

At first, I felt invincible. God had brought me through some challenging years, and He would continue to uphold me as I started down this new path He had for me. I began a Christian

> **Now all glory to God, who is able, through his mighty power at work within us, to accomplish infinitely more than we might ask or think. Glory to him in the church and in Christ Jesus through all generations forever and ever! Amen.**
>
> **—EPHESIANS 3:20–21 (NLT)**

support group at my church for depression, anxiety, and other mental health issues. The group met an important need in our community, and I felt confident in leading the group through Bible studies and exercises to encourage them.

But after a while, I was back on an emotional roller coaster, and this shocked me. Celebrations turned into sorrows, rewards into relapses, and delight into despair. What had happened to being invincible?

"God, You've healed me," I prayed. "My family and friends are my greatest support, and You've brought mental health professionals into my life to help me. I'm leading a support group that I believe You moved me to start. I'm doing everything I can to serve You. So why am I still struggling? Why are my mood swings increasing? Why do I feel so insecure?"

I finally discovered that "doing" God's work had taken the place of "being" in God's presence—even though He walked every step of the way with me. But He did not promise a pain-free life. I live in a broken world. I fight against my sinful nature. And I encounter Satan's attacks. Survival depends on my relationship with the Lord and His promise of an eternal future without worry or pain.

My view of myself as the leader of *my* support group had to change to accepting myself as a participant in *God's* healing work. I began to welcome the support and encouragement I received from group members as we studied God's Word and prayed together for comfort. This verse from 2 Corinthians 1:3–4 (NLT) became a vital part of my life: "All praise to God, the Father of our Lord Jesus Christ. God is our merciful Father and the source of all comfort. He comforts us in all our troubles so that we can comfort others. When they are troubled, we will be able to give them the same comfort God has given us."

A couple of years before my sixtieth birthday, my husband and I downsized and moved to a community farther away from our church. The small-town life I had yearned for finally came to pass. We found a new church home, but I continued leading the support group at our previous church. Eventually, the distance, along with the challenges of 2020, the first year of the COVID-19 pandemic, caused me to end the support group. I wondered what God had in store for me next.

Then a dear friend who had attended the support group called me.

"Caroline, would you be interested in starting a mental wellness group at my church? It's near your home. The pastor is on board and excited about offering the group. What do you think?"

I knew instantly that God had opened the door for me to continue the work He had given me. And I needed the support group as much as anyone.

"Let me pray about it," I answered. "But I can tell you, God is already tugging at my heart to be a part of this ministry."

I have learned to trust in the Lord. Life may not have unfolded in the way that I expected, but peeks into my past reveal that God is always with me. Even when I have doubts or questions, I know His ways are unfathomable and perfect.

The Beautiful Gift of Scars

By Christina Ryan Claypool

Several years ago, I had a suspicious spot on my cheek. As the dermatologist positioned a scalpel-like instrument to take a tissue sample for biopsy, he said, "There will be a scar, but it's better than…"

He paused, not wanting to finish the sentence with the word *cancer*.

"I understand," I said calmly, knowing there was no alternative.

The thirtysomething specialist was about my son's age, causing me to feel motherly protection toward him. Only moments earlier, while he was preparing to examine the moles on my arms, I had warned him, "I used to be a cutter. My left arm is badly scarred."

The young doctor nodded evenly like a seasoned professional. There was no judgment or shock in his youthful brown eyes. Apparently, he was hardened to scars, appreciating their usefulness in the healing process.

Besides the faded evidence of cutting, the dermatologist was about to discover three more serious slashes. Over four decades ago, battling depression and addiction created by childhood trauma, I had cut deeply into my left wrist with a razor blade in a desperate attempt to end my existence. An emergency room physician had carefully stitched the bloody mess back together, but he couldn't fix my broken life. Only Jesus could do that.

It was in 1986 when I miraculously met my marvelous Savior while I was a repeat patient on a psychiatric ward. I had gone through a couple of intentional drug overdoses, which had landed me first in intensive care and then in the psych unit. But during the months of my last hospitalization, the pastors and a few members from a local church had visited me and shared the story of God's love and forgiveness.

More significantly, the senior pastor told me that the distressing trauma I experienced as a child "had hurt God more than it had hurt me." With this new understanding that my pain mattered to my heavenly Father, I invited Jesus into my heart and began to heal emotionally and spiritually.

According to 2 Corinthians 5:17 (NLT), "Anyone who belongs to Christ has become a new person. The old life is gone; a new life has begun!"

I was a "new person" with a "new life," but the scars on my arm reminded me of my hopeless past. I continued to be extremely embarrassed by them and prayed earnestly for God to remove them. Years passed, and although they faded from red to dark pink to white, they never went away.

In all honesty, I was intensely disappointed when the God who can do the miraculous didn't remove these tangible traces of my troubled past. Back then, I lacked understanding about my Creator's resourceful plan to use my scars to validate His constant presence and ongoing healing in my life.

For instance, when I was in my midforties and working as a Christian television reporter, my path crossed with another physician at a local swim club. Unlike my caring dermatologist, this neurologist lacked compassion. He also appeared to have no faith or belief in God. I'm not sure if he was an atheist or agnostic, but he certainly didn't credit our supreme Creator with anything.

"I was committed to a mental institution as a young woman and almost died by suicide," I explained in an effort to share a bit of my testimony. When I told the specialist my story, he acted as if I were lying about my experience.

"People who survive always have scars," the disbelieving doctor countered in an agitated voice. Angrily, he reached for my left arm and turned it sideways to examine it.

His eyes widened and a look of shock settled on his face when he saw the jagged reminders validating what I had just told him. He examined the faded scars running close to the veins in my forearm and the three straight white lines on my wrist stitched neatly back together more than two decades earlier. Seeing the healed reminder of a formerly self-destructive and disturbed young woman, the physician let go of my arm, while reluctantly agreeing the scars corroborated my testimony.

> **As he spoke, he showed them the wounds in his hands and his side. They were filled with joy when they saw the Lord!**
>
> **—JOHN 20:20 (NLT)**

About the same time as my encounter with this medical professional, I met a young Christian man who taught me a valuable lesson about the beauty of scars. Micah tried to take his own life as a teenager by shooting himself. Miraculously, he survived, but his face was dramatically disfigured. Both of our stories of survival were featured in a documentary produced at the TV station where I was then employed.

Our culture would view Micah's scars as an imperfection or an unattractive flaw. Yet in God's economy, this wise survivor taught me that they are a gift, a visible sign of healing and restoration. During our conversation, Micah quoted 1 Peter 4:10 (NLT): "God has given each of you a gift from his great variety of spiritual gifts. Use them well to serve one another." I watched Micah passionately present his gripping testimony as a suicide prevention tool through the documentary and at a church youth group. Through his example, I was inspired to also view my scars as a sacred gift.

Since my encounter with Micah, I take the opportunity to share my story to inspire folks who are ashamed of their scars, whatever form they might be—physical, spiritual, or emotional. Our scars don't have to be disgraceful reminders; instead, they can be victorious spiritual weapons. Our scars display the fact that we survived something destructive, made it to the other side, and God was with us through it all. Once we are healed or in the process of healing, our testimony gives others hope as they journey on their own path to wholeness.

> **The temptations in your life are no different from what others experience. And God is faithful. He will not allow the temptation to be more than you can stand. When you are tempted, he will show you a way out so that you can endure.**
>
> **—1 CORINTHIANS 10:13 (NLT)**

GOD'S GIFT OF TOUCH
— By Eryn Lynum —

WALKING THROUGH A wheat field, you can discover a deeper level of connection with God simply by stretching out your hands. Brushing fingers along wheat blooms allows you to feel the slight friction between your fingertip ridges and the slick stalks and feather-like blossoms. Touching the textiles of nature allows you to draw a conclusion about God: He is multidimensional. He does not see this world or its happenings as flat or linear. Likewise, His children do not experience His presence in a one-dimensional manner. Instead, those He draws near discover a God of many layers.

God's Spirit and grace also continue to be with me during the seasons when depression becomes a battle once again or when the temptation to give into addiction or any kind of self-harm tries to return. At those times, I see my scars as a reminder to keep God by my side and stay in the fight one day at a time. They are confirmation that with the Lord's help, I will get through whatever challenges come my way.

Christians know that the most precious scars are the ones Jesus received while hanging on the cross and giving His life as a ransom for sin. Even after His resurrection when greeting His disciples in a glorified body, Christ's healed wounds remained visible. To me, the Savior's scars are a beautiful representation of the ultimate sacrifice of His ever-present love for His children.

When God Entered My Space

By Dianne Fraser

Mother's Day, when you are a childless woman who wants children, is painfully difficult. Most of the year is hard but do-able, and I had learned all the tricks—avoiding young families, bypassing the baby sections in stores, and keeping busy doing all the fun things a family with children can do.

But Mother's Day is impossible to avoid.

The best doctors in my state had just advised me that the likelihood of my having a child was very remote. They wouldn't say impossible, but the message was clear. When the doctor advised us to "pursue new dreams," my husband and I heard the message loud and clear.

So, I kept busy. However, in a world so focused on the traditional family, the triggers of hurt would come in the most unexpected ways.

To close out the process of my infertility journey, one final surgery was undertaken to repair some of the structural prob-lems uncovered in my treatment. I came home battered and bruised from a significant six-hour operation that was quite overwhelming. To say I felt sorry for myself was an under-statement. The tears came easily, and my heart was heavy. The deepest wound, however, was a poorly timed request for me to serve at church the following week—which, unfortunately, was Mother's Day.

It wasn't a malicious request—just a thoughtless one. And so, despite the weakened physical state of my body and the emotionally fragile state of my heart, I sat on a stool at the doorway of my church and handed out small posies of flowers to every mother who walked through the door that Sunday morning.

And then I went home and sobbed so deeply that eventually I fell into a restless sleep from utter exhaustion.

The following months were hard. I was hurt. I was angry. I didn't understand why God would allow me to long so deeply for a child of my own, yet also give me the

> # I prayed for this child, and the LORD has granted me what I asked of him.
>
> —1 SAMUEL 1:27 (NIV)

physical issues I had. It wasn't fair. I watched achingly as women around me became pregnant time and again—and I tried to celebrate with them in their joy, while seeking to protect my heart. It was a dark and difficult season. Ecclesiastes speaks of there being a time to weep—and this characterized my life. It seemed to be all I did.

Time rolled by, and while my body healed, my heart didn't. It ached for a child. I would awaken in the morning with my arms heavy with need. It was a pain that grew, not lessened, and it was consuming every waking moment of my day. My dreams of being a mother had been reduced to a rubble and the loss was immense. The guilt of not fulfilling my husband's dream of being a dad was also enormous.

It came to a head one rainy day. I was home alone and feeling pretty angry and miserable. I had reached the bottom of my ability to keep going with life this way, and it was time to have it out with God.

After my husband had left for work, I closed the curtains. I turned off the telephone, I lay on my couch, and I sobbed. I told God He couldn't possibly love me if He had allowed this to happen. I said a lot of things to God that were laced with rage. The pressed-down emotions, anger, and fears all bubbled to the surface. I sobbed and eventually whispered, "Do You even care?"

Then God entered my space.

> ## Those who seek the LORD lack no good thing.
>
> **—PSALM 34:10 (NIV)**

The sofa that held my heaving body felt like His arms around me. I could physically sense His presence. I didn't hear a voice or even a whisper, but I knew He was there. And I knew He cared. I knew that He loved me even in this dark space, and that He knew my heart was breaking. And that awareness took the depth of the anger away.

Words of an old hymn "Great Is Thy Faithfulness," by Thomas O. Chisholm, came to mind. Through my tears, I hummed the tune, and then finally the words also came to life in my spirit.

Great is Thy faithfulness, O God my Father,
There is no shadow of turning with Thee;
Thou changest not, Thy compassions, they fail not
As Thou hast been, Thou forever wilt be.

The hymn became a prayer. The words of each chorus became stronger and stronger, until the tears of anger stopped and ones of hope and peace took their place.

Great is Thy faithfulness! Great is Thy faithfulness!
Morning by morning new mercies I see;
All I have needed Thy hand hath provided—
Great is Thy faithfulness, Lord, unto me!

The room was pulsating with the presence of God, and I knew this moment would be one I would never forget.

As the peacefulness of my heart and home came over me, I whispered a prayer that changed everything: "Lord, please grant me the desires of my heart, or take away this longing I feel. I can't battle it any longer."

It was a prayer that wasn't charged with the need for a particular answer, but one in which I genuinely knew I could trust God with His choice for my life. He loved me and He understood—and He would provide for me one way or the other. The words of Lamentations 3:22–23 (ESV) rang true: "The steadfast love of the LORD never ceases; his mercies never come to an end; they are new every morning; great is your faithfulness."

The evidence of this encounter was immediate. I navigated the following weeks with a quiet confidence and peace in my heart. While there were moments of needing to process my infertility during that time, the previously crippling emotions were gone. God had heard my prayer, and His peace and presence walked with me. My erratic cycles no longer caused my heart to catch in nervous anxiety, but instead were met with a sense of acceptance. I found the capacity to smile again.

Six weeks later, following a bout of nausea, the thought came into my head that maybe I was pregnant. I rummaged through the cupboard and found an old pregnancy test to put that thought to rest.

It came up positive! My breath caught in my chest. I told myself to settle down as it could be a false positive—but the five additional tests I performed after a trip to the store all confirmed that a baby was on the way. My husband and I scarcely believed it could be true. My doctors assured me, with wonder in their tones, that this was the case, and put my date of conception down to the very day I encountered God in my living room.

Ecclesiastes speaks of seasons in our lives. I had lived through a time of weeping, mourning, and loss—but as the scriptures state, there is also a time to laugh and dance. I entered a season of celebrating the goodness of God and His miraculous gift of a child. To my joy, the community around us laughed and danced alongside us and communally gave thanks to the faithful God who had answered a prayer as only He could.

God is faithful. Yes, I had a child in my arms and a home to thank Him for—but even more precious was the gift He gave my heart. He is faithful—even when the world looks bleak and cruel—and He will be everything that we need.

Port in the Storm

By Sandi Banks

At last! My heart did the happy dance as our jumbo jet touched down in Chicago, bringing our journey from Warsaw, Poland, to an end…almost.

Two Polish teenagers, Ben and Estella, and I had begun our adventure forty-eight hours earlier, with bumpy European buses, grumpy world travelers, German train delays, international flight layovers, a whirlwind tour of New York City, and more. The teens' parents, Polish ministry friends of mine, wanted their precious children to visit their Canadian aunt and uncle. So I volunteered.

Now, here we were. Mission accomplished!

The aunt and uncle met us with warm smiles and open arms, expressing gratitude in their delightful Polish accents. As we squeezed our weary bodies and heavy luggage into the tiny back seat of their old Honda Civic, I breathed a sigh of relief. In a few hours, the five of us would be in Canada, where I would spend a couple of days in their home before returning to Colorado. At least that was "The Plan," mapped out by the parents before we left Poland.

And it was going swimmingly—until the sixth hour of our drive. While the children slept, the uncle casually announced that we were nearing the Canadian border and that I would not continue with them into Canada after all.

"You must get out here," he said kindly, without explanation. "I am sorry."

I was stunned. *Where is "here"?* I wondered. Through my back-seat window, I could only see night sky and strange surroundings. *Where are we? Where will I go? What will I do?*

With no other arrangement, no funds budgeted for a hotel, and no apparent recourse, I silently cried out. *Lord, please help! Are You going to let them just boot me out in the dark of night? In the middle of nowhere?*

But in that moment, only God knew that I was *not* in the middle of nowhere. I was in the center of His will…in Port Huron, Michigan, home of my dear longtime friend Carol.

Seeing the Port Huron sign, I quickly called Carol's number and heard her welcoming voice. I had barely begun pouring out my plight when she squealed, "Oh, wonderful! Come stay with me!"

Those words ushered in a spontaneous three-day, one-on-one "ministry retreat," orchestrated by the Lord. He had carved out this rare opening in both our busy schedules.

As Carol's husband, Gene, took my luggage up to their son Jason's empty room, Carol and I hugged and marveled at the goodness of God before calling it a night.

I slept like a brick, until the rising Michigan sun and sweet aroma of cinnamon rolls, bacon, and coffee coaxed my jet-lagged body into the new day.

Perched at her kitchen table, Carol and I began chatting like a couple of old school chums, catching up on each other's latest—her son's Naval Academy pursuits, my daughters' activities, and the blessings of God in our whirlwind ministries. Only the warmth of her heart surpassed the warmth of her home. God was very present.

Then my friend's look of delight turned to one of concern as she earnestly asked, "So how are you doing—really?"

Silent tears trickled down my cheeks. A family crisis had shattered my world. I was broken. I needed hope. And God knew I also needed the care of a loving friend to come alongside with fresh reminders that He is the God of all hope.

Two more of Carol's questions set the tone for the rest of our time together.

"What do you suppose God's Word says about that?" she said, reaching for her Bible, as I reached for mine. Together, we began searching the Scriptures. As the pages turned, so did my heart. Peace, encouragement, and comfort began emerging from those pages, offering fresh perspective and rays of hope.

> **Do not be afraid or discouraged, for the LORD will personally go ahead of you. He will be with you; he will neither fail you nor abandon you.**
>
> —DEUTERONOMY 31:8 (NLT)

Her other question, "How shall we pray?" brought healing as it led us into a treasured time with our heavenly Father, pouring out our praises and petitions.

On the third day, we awoke to a gorgeous Sunday morning. I joined Carol and Gene at their church and met many of their friends. I marveled at the way God was using the folks in that local church family to embrace and encourage one another. Clearly, they loved and were being loved by those whom God had placed in their path.

And it seemed He had even handpicked the sermon for me that morning, from the Psalms: "The LORD hears his people when they call to him for help. He rescues them from all their troubles" (Psalm 34:17, NLT).

I left Michigan that afternoon with a deeper love for my God and my friends, and with hope—the hope He had awaiting me on the other edge of the border, the other end of the phone, the other side of the door.

> **For God gave us a spirit not of fear but of power and love and self-control.**
>
> —2 TIMOTHY 1:7 (ESV)

By God's design, I was "booted out" so I could be welcomed in.

But God has even greater plans for you and me beyond getting hope, and that's *giving* hope.

Yes, He knew I needed my praying friend that night, and in the days to follow, more than I needed a drive to Canada to stay with strangers. My plan had been overruled, and I am so grateful. The angel of His presence led me in another direction.

But God also knew something none of us yet knew: The day was coming when a tragic event would turn the lives of those dear friends upside down too. And that I, in turn, would have the privilege of being there for them, as they had been for me, with a heart of love, compassion, and faithful prayers. In the midst of receiving a blessing, I also had been given a clear vision of how I can be a "port in the storm" for another hurting sister.

Corrie ten Boom, the courageous Dutch author, summed it all up beautifully: "Every experience God gives us, every person He puts in our lives, is the perfect preparation for the future that only He can see."

GOD'S GIFT OF SIGHT

— By Lawrence W. Wilson —

TEN VISITORS AT the seaside may come away with ten perspectives on what they saw. One may comment on the vastness of the sea, another on the power of the waves, the variety of wildlife, or the water's greenish hue. One body of water holds infinite secrets. No wonder biblical writers use the ocean as a metaphor for God. He calms the roaring sea (Psalm 65:7), His justice is deep like the ocean (Psalm 36:6), and He hurls our sins into the depths (Micah 7:19). When you've seen all you think there is in the ocean, or the character of God, look again.

Those "experiences" God gives us? Yours may not include crawling into the back seat of a Honda or crying out for a place to stay in the middle of a Michigan night. Yours will involve other challenges—other means of being reminded that God's ways are not always ours; they are higher, and better (see Isaiah 55:9, ESV).

Those people God puts in our lives? Yours may not be a longtime friend or her pastor with a timely message. But whoever God puts in your path will be the perfect preparation for His plan, yet to unfold.

That future that only He can see? Yours may not involve the mending of your broken heart or praying a friend through hers. Your future, and mine, are in the hands of our all-loving God. He will never leave us to face the waves of adversity alone.

We can trust Him to see us through. He is, for you and me, our ever-present Port in the storm.

Miracle Man

By Joann Claypoole

Because he first loved us...

One day last year, my husband, Dennis, texted: "Home soon. Want to go for a walk?"

"You'll be home from work before dark? Wow! That sounds like a New Year's miracle," I replied.

Within minutes, I laced my walking shoes and grabbed the harnesses for our two dogs.

As usual, he came home later than expected—with his phone attached to his ear. I pressed my lips together and gave him the "Are you kidding me" look. He shrugged, turned the iPhone toward me, and his tone changed from loud to semi-aggravated as I read the name of the caller. The all-too-familiar muffled voices of a major client's creative team proved to be the source of another heated conference call. The kind he said never bothered him nor gave him stress—the kind that turned my stomach when I overheard the words.

My mind reeled with thoughts of his hectic schedule and how all the corporate stress had taken its toll before. Only six years earlier, my handsome fifty-nine-year-old husband had suffered a mild stroke. That had motivated me to try to bring more relaxation into our lives. And the following year, I had survived stage-three melanoma. So I was committed even more to work less and play and enjoy life more, and I tried to get him to embark on the relaxation agenda with me.

I imagined us having fun with our grandchildren, hiking, boating, off-road jeeping, and enjoying sunset dinners on our cabin's porch for many years to come. He envisioned taking his company to new heights of success while doing all these other things too.

We never did go for the walk that early January evening. He started experiencing upper back pain and mild chest pressure, so I went into commando mode. "You've already had a stroke. Get in the Jeep. We're going to the hospital."

I knew something was terribly wrong when he didn't refuse.

Within the hour, I watched in terror as Dennis suffered a massive heart attack in the emergency room of our local hospital. *This can't be happening. He said he was fine a few minutes ago—*

> **You make known to me the path of life; in your presence there is fullness of joy; at your right hand are pleasures forevermore.**
>
> **—PSALM 16:11 (ESV)**

"We'll have to take it moment by moment." The doctor's soft-spoken words were difficult to accept as he explained that Dennis had already flatlined several times. "I'll do everything I can to save him, but without a miracle, he won't survive. Your husband's brain and other organs have likely sustained severe damage, but it is evident he is a well-loved man. We should all be so blessed to have such prayers lifted on our behalf. Tonight, his life is in our true Healer's hands."

His words repeated in my mind as our pastor held hands with my son and me and led our family in prayer right there in the crowded ER hallway.

Once again, even in this most wicked storm of our lives, we leaned on one of our Heavenly Father's faithful promises: *I am with you always.* We believed that promise with all our hearts because he loved us first—with all of His heart.

> **Seek the LORD and his strength; seek his presence continually!**
>
> —PSALM 105:4 (ESV)

Nurses, patients, and random people bowed their heads in prayer too. My four sons and I clung to one another in the hallway until the blur of activity settled. One hour seemed like an eternity. Most of the emergency room crew stopped working on him and walked out from behind the teal curtain.

I didn't realize that this might be my final chance to let him know I couldn't let him go. I only knew I had to see him, if only to touch his face once more.

Beeping monitors quieted. A nurse opened the curtain and took my hand. "You can have a few moments." Her smile warmed my aching heart, but her face was ashen with a hint of sadness. "Think positive thoughts. Believe he'll hear you, and he will."

I prayed that he felt my kiss as my salty tears fell. Fear gripped my throat and threatened to crush all my tomorrows, but after the doctor motioned me to move closer, I leaned down to whisper in Dennis's ear. I kissed his face and watched as one rogue tear slid down his cheek.

"Don't leave us. I love you. We need you. Please. Stay with us." The words fell from my mouth as I held back gut-wrenching sobs. I didn't know if he heard me, but his pulse went from eighteen to sixty, and then they rushed him to the cath lab.

In those terrifying moments, I cried aloud to the Lord, and I felt his presence. I witnessed how God moved mountains in that emergency room to send forth another testimony of His grace and mercy.

It wasn't even about us. This moment was about a God who hears his children. The one who already conquered death once and for all heard my heart's cry. He is the Lord of miracles who sees and gives and loves with everything within Him. His constant presence is my strong, faithful anchor.

Dennis awoke from sedation four days later. Monitors and tubes filled almost every inch of the room. Tears streamed down my face as I watched him struggle to speak. When I leaned closer, he said, "I love you, baby…I'm so sorry," as if he knew the terrors I had witnessed and the possibilities of what else our family might endure.

That evening, he told a vivid story of the light that had surrounded him, of the beautiful purple water he found himself in, and how lyrical voices and serene instrumentals led him upstream—and somehow, back to us.

God heard our prayers and showed us He alone can make a way where there is no way, and only He can give life and breath back to the dead.

Pneumonia, heparin intolerance, blood clots, A-fib, and a transfusion followed, but somehow, Dennis grew stronger. He walked farther. I prayed every day and night. *Thank You, God, for answering our prayers.*

My hubby remained in the CVICU for two weeks before he was stable enough for triple bypass surgery. Emergency room nurses stopped by daily to say hello and encourage his progress. A few mentioned how they shared the news about the guy who had a heart attack that lasted over an hour and survived—without any lingering organ damage.

"Surely, God's not done using Dennis," they said.

Like me, his doctors and nurses knew something supernatural had happened…People referred to him as the Miracle Man.

Although I'd rather learn from times of joy, I've seen how God proved His love over and over during our darkest nights. There are many reasons to be thankful, even for ugly scars and the trauma of the worst days of our lives. While I believe we witnessed several miracles during Dennis's hospital stay, I know there's only one miracle man. His name is Jesus: the Son and Image of the one true God who not only gives and takes away; He's the Great Physician who nurtures, heals, and loves us.

Whenever fear, anger, or sorrow crash into our lives like a hurricane, we only need to look up to the heavens—to the one who steers the wind, the waves, and doctors' hands. His constant presence gives us peace, strength, and hope.

Overwhelming Peace
in His Presence

By Katie R. Dale

My husband and I sat in the hospital parking lot, anxiously waiting for a maternity ward nurse to admit us. Even though I was in labor, the COVID-19 pandemic had recently struck the world, and we had to be checked for fevers before entering the hospital.

No matter how excited we were, we had to follow this new health-care protocol. Here we were at a precipice—our first-born, a boy, would be in our arms soon. We couldn't have been more exhilarated. Although our family members could not be with us, we had each other. What a historic time to have a baby!

My birthing plan was to "play it by ear." I wasn't sure how COVID-19 would affect us, but I anticipated treating the labor and delivery process like a marathon. As a longtime runner, I knew I needed to call on my endurance, pace myself, and be ready for change.

And it certainly was a marathon. After twenty-one hours of contractions, an epidural, and other aids, my body was finally ready for me to start pushing. I fought another four-hour fight to bring our son into the world.

However, that wasn't the finish line.

When they placed our baby, Jaxon, on my chest, I knew my son was not OK. His wet, limp body turned blue in the six seconds they rubbed him down. The charge nurse then cut the cord quickly to whisk him to the warming table.

Several nurses hovered over me, while others fought to resuscitate our baby. I told my husband, Chris, we should pray.

"God, please give us a miracle. Breathe life into our baby boy," Chris pleaded.

Chris and I had waited ten years to start a family, and now it looked as if our firstborn was being taken from us. Yet, there was a lack of emotional upheaval in my heart. Instead, I felt an overwhelming sense of peace that surpassed my understanding of what was happening, just as Philippians 4:7 describes.

Twenty-three minutes after his birth, Jaxon's lungs filled with breath, and he was stabilized on a ventilator. We continued praying, hoping for a miracle. For four days, a special hypothermia cooling treatment was performed on Jaxon to preserve his brain function. Then, an MRI was ordered. However, Chris had reservations. He worried there would be a chance of Jaxon's ventilator possibly disconnecting on the way to the MRI. Chris looked to me uncertainly, conflicted about the risk.

"What do you think we should do?" he said.

I encouraged him, recognizing the step of faith we had to take in this moment. "He'll be fine either way. But if we want the answers the MRI will provide, we have to do this."

During our wait for the MRI results, Chris and I waited in the lobby. I paced back and forth around the chairs. "This is like being on the brink. Maybe Jaxon will come through. We'll get answers to his condition and who knows—maybe we'll get to take him home." I sputtered expressions of hope.

The next day we met with the neurologist in Jaxon's nursery. The sound of our six-day-old son's heartbeat tracing beeped in the background, signaling his prompted breathing cadences.

After the neurologist examined our son, he began. "Mr. and Mrs. Dale, I looked through the MRI results, and they indicate that he has no brain activity. He's gone. I'm so very sorry."

He further explained that seizure activity had happened moments after his birth, and that his brain function had been compromised with only basic brain stem responses remaining. Apparently, a blood condition I have may have made him susceptible to brain damage and complications when the vacuum was applied to his head during delivery.

> **Many waters cannot quench love, neither can floods drown it.**
>
> —SONG OF SOLOMON 8:7 (ESV)

This was an abrupt halt in our march to victory. Our family and friends had all been praying and hoping for a miracle, expecting Jaxon to make it. The anchor we had grasped—hope—suddenly seemed displaced.

My faith hit a brick wall. My heart fought to embrace what my mind already acknowledged—Jaxon was not going home. I wanted so much to believe God would perform a miracle. After all, we had prayed earnestly.

The only other thing such a trial could test was my love for my son. In such a time of tragedy, this little baby's life taught me to love without inhibition. I needed to fight the urge to withdraw from him to protect my heart and emotions, and I needed to be vulnerable. Even as the worst unfolded, love was the answer. So, instead of shuttering my heart to the gravity of this tragedy, I opened the doors of my heart. Wide.

While Jaxon reposed like a doll in our arms, Chris and I sang him soothing lullabies. We stood over his bedside for hours, stroking his head, washing his pale skin, combing his wisps of hair, and wiping away the bubbles coming from the ventilator in his mouth. We moistened his lips when they dried and cracked. With soft strips of gauze, we caught tears from his eyes and preserved them. We smelled his baby scent. We changed his diapers.

> **But Jesus said, "Let the little children come to me and do not hinder them, for to such belongs the kingdom of heaven."**
>
> —MATTHEW 19:14 (ESV)

We cherished the time we had with Jaxon. Every morning at the time he had been born, we celebrated another birthday. We read to him from the Bible and other books. We told him about Jesus and each of his family members. We told him about ourselves, what our lives were like, who we were. We loved him for every second of those eight days, until it was time to say goodbye.

For Jaxon's final day with us, we were allowed to hold him close, without IVs and other hookups—the way we should have all along. Within the privacy of the room we lodged in at the NICU, we took turns holding him, walking him around the room, and lying down in the bed. We kissed his sweet, soft cheeks, caressed his head full of hair, and savored every second we had together.

He breathed short, gasping breaths the last seventeen hours off the ventilator. It pained us to hear his breathing become raspier and include more gurgles from the fluids filling his lungs. The agony of this reality set us into survival mode. We stayed up through the night, crying, singing, praying, and battling the shadows of the valley we were in. It felt like a carousel ride I couldn't get off. I wanted it to stop, but I didn't want his life to end.

While we wished things to go back two weeks—before COVID, before labor and delivery, before sliding into this incoherent, foreign world—time marched on. Before nine o'clock in the morning the following day, Jaxon took his last breath in my arms.

And instead of devastation, there was peace—overwhelming peace, knowing that he was now in Jesus's presence, rejoicing in eternal life with our Savior. We took comfort in that promise that "for to such belongs the kingdom of heaven" (Matthew 19:14, ESV). We began to accept this new reality, which was completely unexpected as we drove home without our baby in the car seat.

During the NICU stay, we invited as many friends as possible to pray for him. We saw that Jaxon's fight to live was a mighty movement of God, one that awakened the urge to pray in those friends and family who may not have experienced that prompting otherwise.

Jaxon's life and passing taught us the biggest lesson in life— love is a risk worth taking. Now we open our hearts, no matter the circumstances, no matter how closed off the world is, because only an open heart can let love in and let love out.

Chance opportunities are
really consequences of
courageous acts of faith,
conscious decisions to
believe that good things
can and will happen.

—Mary Alice Monroe, author

CHAPTER 4

Chance Encounters that Transformed Lives

A Day of God's Wonders

By Karan Koelling

As I drove through the rural landscape that December afternoon, my thoughts were as dreary as the scene around me. The river that ran alongside our highway was frozen and lined with brown, naked trees and dormant pastures.

My husband, Arden, and I had been thrust into our own winter season, complete with a blizzard of challenges. Arden had been diagnosed with dementia that had progressed quickly. My hip ached constantly, aggravated by a house with too many stairs. While the scenery around us was stark, our own future seemed bleak.

That morning, Arden and I had struggled to carry six heavy packs of floor tiles from the laundry room to our silver Impala. We'd had a new floor installed and were returning unused tiles for a refund, even though we'd have to drive sixty-five miles for that errand.

We headed south on a ribbon of two-lane highway nestled between fields where cattle grazed on corn stubble. Arden was dozing by the time we drove through the first village on our route. His chin drooped on his chest, his favorite red Nebraska Cornhuskers cap perched snugly on his head.

Oh, how I love this man. Arden's kind eyes and contagious smile had lifted my spirits for many years. Despite the disease's progress, that hadn't changed.

Dementia was robbing Arden of his memories, though. He had no frame of reference to initiate a conversation. That meant no more heart-to-heart conversations with my dearest friend. I was losing him more and more every day.

With an unsure future, we looked to our grown kids. Over Thanksgiving, they'd helped us list our split-level house with a Realtor, but we hadn't found anything that suited our future needs yet. Worse, I needed additional surgery on my hip.

> **Listen to this, Job; stop and consider God's wonders.**
>
> —JOB 37:14 (NIV)

Why was life so difficult? We were only in our midseventies.

An image came to my mind of a painting I'd chosen years earlier. In the painting, a path wound through a dense, dark forest where a beam of light streamed from above. Arden had hung it in a place where we'd see it every day—above our fireplace. Printed below the painting were the words, "Cast your cares on the LORD and he will sustain you; he will never let the righteous be shaken" (Psalm 55:22, NIV).

In that quiet car, with eyes on the road ahead, I asked God to take up my burdens and to protect us that day.

When Arden's eyes popped open, I greeted him. "Hi, handsome! We're almost there. Are you OK?"

"Yes," he said as he smiled. "I'm with my honey."

After parking in a handicapped space, we entered the sprawling hardware store and signed refund papers in the flooring section. By this time, Arden was exhausted and decided to wait for me in the car.

I was tired too. And my hip felt like it was on fire. I straightened my shoulders, though, determined to make it to the next stop at the customer service department.

The lady behind the counter looked at my refund papers. She was all business. "Since you originally paid in cash, the store policy is for the refund to be in cash," she said, matter-of-factly. She counted out seven hundred–dollar bills, laying them on the L-shaped counter in front of me.

> **Have I not commanded you? Be strong and courageous. Do not be afraid; do not be discouraged, for the LORD your God will be with you wherever you go.**
>
> —JOSHUA 1:9 (NIV)

I was instantly wary. A clean-cut young man in his late teens stood nearby, watching. He appeared to be in a hurry.

"I'll be back later," he said to the clerk.

I didn't notice much about him. But I was worried that he knew I held a large amount of cash in my trembling hands—hands that would require a walker as I navigated my way back to our car.

Uneasy, I grasped my walker with both hands, while trying to hold the refund papers and my clutch purse. I searched the perimeter of the store as I left but saw no one. Hobbling across the parking lot, I hurried toward our car as quickly as my tired body and painful hip allowed. Cold, winter air nipped my exposed fingers. It was late afternoon, and everything was quiet in a normally busy parking lot.

I saw Arden up ahead in the car waiting for me. I struggled to better grasp my purse, but it was hard enough to navigate with my walker. After what felt like hours, I'd almost reached the car and was ready to sigh in relief.

Suddenly a body swooped from behind me. With a sudden, powerful lunge, the person snatched the clutch purse and papers.

I watched, stunned, as a tall, dark-haired, teenage boy raced across the parking lot with my purse. For a moment, I stood dazed and speechless. Finally, I shouted. "Help! I've been robbed!"

Three people outside the garden center heard my cry. A man in his forties and his son chased the thief. By the time I reached the garden center, a young woman had already called the police.

The man and his son returned from the chase, unable to apprehend my attacker. "I saw him jump into a 2002 blue Silverado pickup. He had an accomplice. I'm sorry. I didn't get close enough to see the license plate."

He asked how much money was in my purse, and I explained I'd just received a refund of $725.

The three witnesses didn't hesitate. "We'll wait here to give a report to the police."

In the meantime, Arden had spotted us from the car and joined us to find out what had happened. A sales associate ushered Arden and me to chairs inside the store, where he offered us bottled water.

When the investigating officer finished questioning the witnesses, he came inside to interview me about my purse and its contents. As we talked, I realized how grim our situation had become. We hadn't only been robbed of a significant refund, but my driver's license and credit cards were also gone. How would we get home?

"I no longer have a credit card or cash to pay for gas to get home. There's a checkbook in our car, but now I don't have a driver's license for identification."

"I can get your license number from the DMV," the officer said. "There's a gas station at the end of this strip mall. I'll make arrangements and escort you there."

As Arden and I returned to our car, we were surprised to see the young woman who'd called the police. She greeted us with a warm smile.

"I have something for you," she said.

When I saw the folded check in her hand, I protested. "Oh, thank you. But no. We'll be OK."

"I want to do this. Here," she said, pressing the check into my hand. "Don't open it until I'm gone." She softly added, "God bless you."

After she'd left, we opened the check, written for $700. Such generosity from a total stranger overwhelmed our hearts.

Officer Woods returned and accompanied us to the nearby gas station. He handed me a paper containing my driver's license number. After I paid for the gas with a check, he pumped our gas.

By the time we left the city, a lovely sunset graced the sky in pink and peach hues. Instead of grieving our loss, Arden and I basked in the warm afterglow of kindness we'd experienced. Even the sky affirmed God's goodness through strangers. It overwhelmed this hateful act of robbery. What had begun as a worry-filled day had become warm and sweet. We'd received gifts of comfort, provision, and help when we'd least expected them.

That December evening, after eating bowls of hot soup, Arden and I lingered at our kitchen table where we examined the check we'd received from Kaylee, our young friend. In the

GOD'S GIFT OF SIGHT
— By Eryn Lynum —

WATCHING A CATERPILLAR retreat into its cocoon, one might wonder how much the creature knows. In the coming days, enzymes will break down cells in the organs, muscles, and digestive system. Its old body is done away with so it can become new. Would it dare to enter its chrysalis if the caterpillar understood what was coming? Hebrews 11:1 (NIV) says, "Now faith is confidence in what we hope for and assurance about what we do not see." Observing a butterfly flit from flower to flower, the unknowns become obsolete. In timely glimpses of His plans, God tucks an intuitive faith into His children's hearts— one that will usher them into incredible transformation.

---

top left-hand corner were printed the words "Consider God's Wonders."

God had given us a glimpse of His faithfulness when circumstances screamed devastation.

Arden continued to decline, going from hospital to hospital. He died on my birthday. I discovered that as bad as the robbery was, it was nothing compared to what I faced in the death of my husband.

But God had been with me already on another dark, winter day of my soul, proving His ability to care for and protect me. He had confirmed to my heart that His wonders would overcome any difficulty I faced. He'd turn the darkest day into a glorious sunset.

Peace Instead of Panic

By Delores Liesner

What a waste of time and money, I thought, reading the denial letter from the organization that ran the senior exercise program. Though my application and payment were accepted because I was over seventy, I'd been denied access unless I could provide a doctor's permission slip that included my current pulse and blood pressure.

I knew my primary doctor would insist on an appointment for that, for which I'd have to pay, so I called my chiropractor, who told me to come to his office for the quick numbers at no charge.

The pulse was no issue, but the staff member was getting anxious as she took my blood pressure over and over. She first used the automatic arm cuff, then a larger cuff, and then a manual cuff. Then she tried them all over again. She left the room and came back with the doctor, who said, "The problem is not with the machines—it is your numbers. The lowest of all the attempts was 246 over 158! This is a medical emergency."

I just looked at him in shock.

"You must listen to me and go right to an emergency room," he continued. "You should not even be driving."

He had me try to call my husband, Ken, to come and get me, but I couldn't get through. I told the doctor I felt fine, but he made me promise to drive slowly home and have Ken drive me to the hospital.

On the way to the hospital, I reviewed all I'd heard or read about blood pressure—the "silent killer," as it was called.

Well, I thought, *it is possible that this is it for me even though I feel no pain. If it is, I want Your peace, Lord. To honor You in life or in death.*

I thought of John 14:27 (NASB): "Peace I leave you; My peace I give you; not as the world gives, do I give to you. Do not your heart be troubled, nor fearful."

My mind latched onto that single word—*peace*—and peace became my prayer. As I began repeating my simple prayer of peace, Ken pulled the car up to the emergency room.

> # Then you will experience God's peace, which exceeds anything we can understand. His peace will guard your hearts and minds as you live in Christ Jesus.
>
> **—PHILIPPIANS 4:7 (NLT)**

After I signed in, nurses took my blood pressure again, and it had only dropped a few numbers. I knew if I thought too much about what poking and prodding might come next, the numbers would only increase. While they discussed my plight, I kept softly praying, *Peace. Peace.* And I felt God's presence and His peace.

A cardiologist introduced himself while several other staff members circled my bed and went into action, hooking me up to a blood pressure cuff, inserting an IV, taking information, and softly discussing the numbers as the doctor questioned me on why I didn't appear stressed.

He shook his head and said, "You are sitting there calm as can be, and these are very dangerous numbers."

He asked about stress in my life, and I explained that I was involved with caregiving for a relative, as well as being a writer and speaker. He asked what I wrote and spoke about.

> **Trust in the LORD forever, for the LORD, the LORD himself, is the Rock eternal.**
>
> **—ISAIAH 26:4 (NIV)**

I told about my testimony—finding purpose despite an abusive past and writing about the miracles that happened after I turned my life over to Christ.

"Well, you certainly don't seem stressed right now," he commented, looking perplexed. He ordered one medicine intravenously, which made the numbers go up instead of down, then tried another, which only worked temporarily, so he said I would have to go to the ICU.

"I am going to let your pressure down slowly," he explained.

"You are going to let me down already and we only just met?" I joked.

The doctor chuckled and shook his head. "We don't often laugh in here," he commented. "We've never had someone like you before."

Ken was teary as my bed was rolled into the ICU, where I was hooked up to several machines. Then the fun began!

I still felt peaceful and was silently communicating with God. Nurses and assistants came in and out of the room, explaining all the tests that would be done. Every one of them said they heard I was a writer and speaker and asked what I wrote and spoke about.

After a half dozen of those questions, I asked my husband to run home, call a few people to pray, and get some copies of my book that I could share, as well as some booklets that explained about faith.

More medication was administered through the IV, and I continued to pray, *Peace. Peace.* The blood pressure dropped quickly—so quickly that I thought I was having a heart attack. And then more peace descended. Ken returned with the materials, relieved to see the lower numbers on the monitor.

We were giving thanks to God that my numbers had improved when more staff came in to explain x-rays, ultrasounds, scans, and treatments that would be done that day and the next. The hospital grapevine was apparently quite active as each entering medical helper told me he or she heard I had a published book and asked about my writing, my faith, and my peace prayer. Every one of them eagerly accepted the material Ken brought from home, and Ken and I watched as God's presence filled the room. What we had expected to be a somber time was remarkably joyful.

In between x-rays and scans, I assured Ken that I was fine and that this might be a good time to visit his brother in a nearby nursing home, and to bring more books and materials from home.

On the third day in the hospital, a doctor told me that every one of my tests was unremarkable. He chuckled. "Even though your tests are unremarkable, you are a remarkable patient," he said. "It looks like you'll live a long time to continue sharing your stories."

Faith Blossoms

By Nancy Hoag

"Those flowers will never grow there," the elderly man said.

He shook his head like the high school algebra teacher who never did figure out that creative writing was my thing, and that numbers just went over my head. Meanwhile, this stately, silver-haired man I did not know had more than once paced back and forth in front of our RV that morning. He had also wordlessly watched me kneel and diligently work with the difficult soil and wilting plants. And now here he was again. Hovering, shrugging, and this time announcing, "I'm a retired botanist..."

A retired botanist? Why hadn't he appeared before I'd driven all the way across town and purchased every bedding plant my heart desired, along with bags of potting soil? And why was he only now volunteering this information? Had I even asked for his opinion?

I made myself smile as I politely thanked him, but he was a bit late with his unsolicited knowledge.

"Well," I said, "I'll be hoping, anyway—" And, hoping was the word. Not just about these flowers but also because my husband's health had given us a recent scare. Not only had he been dealing with cancer, but his diabetes had also begun to give him trouble. I'd tried not to focus on the negative; my husband needed me to be encouraging and optimistic. My focusing on the gorgeous flowers I anticipated blossoming would help me be encouraging and optimistic. I loved flowers, and I loved my husband, and I also trusted that God would fill our miniature flowering bed to overflowing.

I nodded at the botanist. "Hoping," I said, more for my hearing than for his. And that was all I said because just as soon as this professional had said what he obviously believed I needed to hear, he'd turned back toward to his own park model, where not one single flower had been planted. A lone, prickly cactus—nothing with even an ounce of joy or color.

"So, now what?" I breathed. The RV slot we'd rented had turned out to be so much less than what we'd anticipated. The online ad had made it sound charming.

"Disappointing," I said in a phone call to a friend who'd been certain we would thoroughly enjoy our winter in a climate much warmer than our home in Montana. Meanwhile, because we'd prepaid in full for our space, we'd made up our minds to stay put in this retirement village for at least three, maybe four, months. Furthermore, I had made up my mind about no grumbling. *Be grateful,* I reminded the part of me that longed to whine.

"So, Father," I said. "I thank You for giving us this opportunity to come away from a bitter and chilling winter. I ask You please to bless these beautiful buds and blossoms."

Grabbing my camera, I took several shots to send back home. Shaking the dirt from my gloves, I headed back inside for an iced tea and to grab the journal I'd been keeping. I would note the date and the names of all the flowers, and I would continue to praise God for not only today's miniature blossoms but also for the abundance I anticipated.

The following week, the botanist walked by again, planted himself where he could stare at my recently planted bed, and shook his head.

> "The LORD is my portion," says my soul, "therefore I will hope in him."
>
> —LAMENTATIONS 3:24 (ESV)

"They might look good today," he said, shrugging. "But they're not going to last. Might hang on for a couple more days, but then—"

I smiled and respectfully nodded. I wasn't going to argue, nor did I feel it appropriate to tell him I had prayed. There would be no point in telling him this flower bed was now in God's hands.

Several more weeks went by while I watered, fertilized, and delighted in my amazing flowers. I admittedly worried some that I'd wake up one morning and discover everything would have either withered or disappeared completely, but daily I discovered that what I'd prayed over was actually thriving and becoming more beautiful by the hour.

Then one morning when I hadn't seen him coming, the botanist appeared. The day hadn't yet begun for most of my neighbors, but I had taken my Bible and devotionals out to the patio for the quiet I needed. I had silently prayed and thanked God for my thriving garden. Now with my coffee in hand and the warming sun on my back, I'd been looking even more closely at how "God's garden" was doing when the botanist didn't simply walk by—he waved. And this time he was coming even closer to stare at the dazzling plantings that filled my flower bed with bountiful blessings. With a puzzled expression, he nodded, shook his head, and without uttering one single word, he continued his walk. But I knew he had been amazed. He wouldn't say so, but the garden that shouldn't have been planted wasn't simply in full bloom but spilling over the rim of the concrete enclosure.

Meanwhile, as the day progressed, park residents and visitors alike strolled by, stopped, studied my flowers, and shook their heads. One woman sang, "How lovely." Another exclaimed, "They're gorgeous!" A third asked, "How did you get them to grow so large?"

> **But let patience have its perfect work, that you may be perfect and complete, lacking nothing.**
>
> —JAMES 1:4 (NKJV)

"I prayed," I said. "The Lord did this."

The woman smiled. "Yes," she said. "He does all things well…"

I nodded. "All things well…"

I breathed in deeply. Yes, my husband had been dealing with both cancer and diabetes. And, yes, I'd been grieving for the family we hadn't seen in far too long. In addition, my work as a freelance writer hadn't been going all that well. "Impossible," I'd said too many times over the past year with regard to my family *and* my husband's health *and* the work that seemed as if it would never bear fruit. But today the flowers that would "never grow there" *were* growing there.

The chance encounter with the "professional" had actually become, for me, a challenge. He'd unknowingly sent me back to God's Word. And now, with proof that we humans can't always understand nor even imagine His workings, God had grown an "impossible" garden.

GOD'S GIFT OF SIGHT

— By Tez Brooks —

THE OPTIC NERVE contains more than a million nerve cells. Those, along with millions of rods and cones, help the human brain distinguish shapes and ten million different colors. The eye is the fastest muscle in the body, contracting in less than 1/100th of a second. In fact, because the eye can focus on up to fifty different objects per second, 80 percent of all learning comes through sight. The human eye is truly a unique and complex organ, allowing us to behold the beauty of God's creation.

He had also tucked inside my heart the measure of faith I needed in order to fully believe my husband's cancer battle was in His hands, and He would not be defeated. The painful estrangement from the family members I loved dearly was also not an impossible situation for God; He knew exactly how to cause a family to flourish. I could trust Him for the reconnection. And my work? He had called me. I knew that if those flowers had not only survived but prospered, then I would not only keep going but also growing.

The professional botanist couldn't have imagined how his curt words would become a blessing. Our God, in His own time, perfected what might have seemed impossible. And I would continue to plant words on paper and trust that I was growing and that my work would, in God's own time, blossom as well.

God, You Want Me to Do What?

By Tim Bennett

"You're number one!"

I couldn't believe what the man on the phone was telling me—even though I had prayed about the results of the writing contest nonstop for months, this was unexpected. My wife, Veronique, and I had recently moved to the south of France as missionaries with Youth With A Mission (YWAM), so I was focused on other things now.,

I was number one. My entry had been chosen over almost one thousand other submissions for the top literary prize for the national Amy Awards. But not only did I win the top honor, but I also won $10,000 for the article and would be flown out to Lansing, Michigan, to receive the check in person. How awesome was that!

But now I had another problem.

What do I do with all that money?

Ideas swirled through my brain for the next several days— we could put down a deposit on a house, buy a new car, or take an exotic vacation. However, each time I told my wife, Veronique, of my new idea, she was unmoved. "No, I don't think that's it."

Finally, I figured it was time to pray.

God answered in the same way that He encouraged me to enter the contest—with a question. For the contest, He had said, "Why not Tim Bennett?" In reference to the money, He said, "Why don't you adopt another child?"

This was not what I expected. I was forty-eight, and Veronique and I had already adopted two children, Alicia and Samuel, now ages ten and seven. I couldn't see adding another child this late in life. In fact, I thought my hands were pretty full just working full-time and refereeing sibling disputes. Surely I was missing the Lord's message on this one. For confirmation, I asked Veronique what she thought of my latest idea. Surprisingly, she smiled and said, "You know, that's the first thing you've said that appeals to me."

I was not fully convinced, however. I needed further confirmation. Like Gideon, I decided to cast a fleece before the Lord. *Lord, if this is from You to adopt another child, please confirm it at the evangelical conference in Budapest, Hungary, that we'll be attending next month.*

I figured I was pretty safe. After all, how many missionary conferences talk about adoption? Months before, when Veronique and I registered, we had signed up for some classes on how to start a new church. When we arrived at the conference, however, we were shocked to discover that the church planting track had been canceled and a new seminar had been added—"International Adoptions."

Intrigued, we went to the first session, and I told the presenter about casting our fleece before the conference. She burst out, "Praise the Lord! That's God for you!"

To be frank, her zeal and confidence scared me. I mean, this was easy for her to say. She could chalk up another adoption and pocket some more money. On the other hand, if this was

God speaking to me, my whole life was about to change—permanently. I felt like I was a wallflower being shoved out onto the dance floor while hanging on to the pillar of the way things were.

This was getting serious. I had to be sure, didn't I? I told the Lord after the conference, "This is all very interesting, but before we make such a decision that will affect all our lives so dramatically, could you please confirm this through your Word?" I thought of the verse: "So then faith *comes* by hearing, and hearing by the word of God" (Romans 10:17, NKJV). If I ever needed a word from God to give me faith to make this radical step, it was now.

> Trust in the LORD with all your heart and lean not on your own understanding; in all your ways submit to him, and he will make your paths straight.
>
> —PROVERBS 3:5–6 (NIV)

After I uttered that prayer, I forgot all about it until one Sunday when my family and I attended a church we'd never visited before. We had not been in France long and wanted to check out the local ministries before committing ourselves to one body of believers. I remember this evangelical church was small, like many in France, and the pastor was juggling all the parts of the service himself, including the announcements, the worship, the offering, and the sermon. He said his text was from the Gospel of John.

As I opened my Bible to the verse, my eyes wandered to the next page and this verse popped out to me: "I will not leave you as orphans; I will come to you" (John 14:18, NIV). This was no coincidence. I knew it was God's confirmation that we should adopt another child.

> **There is a time for everything, and a season for every activity under the heavens.**
>
> —ECCLESIASTES 3:1 (NIV)

The next thing we did was get in touch with the Christian organization from the conference and got the wheels moving for an international adoption. We prayed and talked with our children and decided to adopt a child from Ukraine. When we got to Kyiv, we were blessed to have an exceptional group of Ukrainian young people from the organization to help us with the process. We went to the adoption office and were given a huge binder that had photos of hundreds of children available for adoption. It was overwhelming to see so many children in need of families. When we saw a six-year-old boy's sad face, we both immediately felt compassion for him and felt convinced he was God's choice for us.

We told the lady in charge that he was our boy. She looked at the photo and said, "I'm sorry, but another couple has already selected him. They were looking for a girl but didn't find one, so they picked him instead. You'll need to choose someone else."

My wife and I were convinced that he was the one, so with Veronique's approval, I said, "We will wait for a day or so and pray that the couple will find a girl they can adopt."

Sure enough, the next day we were told the couple had found a girl, and we were free to adopt our Jonathan. Our children were thrilled to have a new brother, and our son, Samuel, loved putting him on his shoulders at the orphanage and parading around the visiting room to Jonathan's obvious delight. It took time for them to communicate clearly with him since Jonathan only spoke Ukrainian, but within a year he could get his points across in both English and French.

If we had any doubts that we had the right child, they were forever laid to rest once we got back to the United States. Veronique had picked up a book in which the author revealed that she had adopted a child from a foreign country. Veronique gave me the book to read and I came across a passage that blew me away.

I asked Veronique, "Did you notice the day that this author's adopted child was born?"

"No. What?"

"December 4—the same day as Jonathan."

God was present through the entire adoption process, and He honored my request for more signs and confirmations as the days went by. I learned that God understands my emotional struggles sometimes in doing His will and will gladly make His will known if I can only surrender my own understanding and trust in Him to show me—whether it be through my inner convictions and peace, through others, through His Word, or a combination of these things.

A Visit from the Fire Department

By Kathryn Sadakierski

The April evening was cool, crisp, and perfect for a stroll, so my parents, sister, and I decided to go for a walk around the neighborhood. Stars stretched across the heavens, except where hidden by errant clouds. Even so, a bright shaft of moonlight illuminated our path.

We figured our walk would be brief, so we left our cell phones at home, reasoning that we wouldn't need them. Being outside was a balm for our spirits, during this difficult time. My paternal grandfather had passed away days before, and the sting of loss was fresh.

Taking family walks is a regular part of our routine. At this time, the coronavirus pandemic was unfolding, and we needed this sense of normalcy to keep us together as other aspects of life transformed around us. With every breath of fresh air we inhaled, a worry died away like a candle flame tapering into evaporating smoke.

Several minutes later, when we returned from our walk, we decided to extend our time outside and sit on our backyard patio. We'd had many a conversation threaded with laughter as we gazed at the constellations in this space. We barely noticed the moments ticking by.

Finally, we went to the garage to let ourselves back into the house. We clicked on the garage door remote. The door did not budge. We each took turns trying to open it, figuring that one of us would have the magic touch. Perhaps something was blocking the door inside? Were we standing too close to the door? Did we need to try holding the remote in a different position? There seemed to be a million possibilities as to what was off-kilter.

Regardless of how we attempted to troubleshoot the issue, we still were shivering outside. We finally determined that the battery needed to be replaced. *Would we be remaining under the stars all through this chilly night?* we wondered.

Typically, we'd have left at least one door or window unlocked while at home, but tonight, we'd closed the house up tightly. After unsuccessfully trying every possible entry, we realized that we had no alternate way into the house. We had no access to the batteries we'd need for the remote and nothing that could help us open a door or window. Our keys were locked inside the house. We hadn't expected to need a spare key for a short walk.

Without our cell phone, we couldn't contact anyone, and it being night, we couldn't go to our neighbors for help. Every house in the neighborhood was dark—not one light was shining in a window.

Dad decided to walk to the nearby gas station to use their phone, but the walk would be treacherous as he passed along

> **See, I am sending an angel ahead of you to guard you along the way and to bring you to the place I have prepared.**
>
> —EXODUS 23:20 (NIV)

a road that was busy and dangerous, especially at night. I was worried and frustrated, continually revisiting "if onlys"—*If only I had brought the phone. If only we had gone out earlier. If only one of us had stayed home.*

> **Therefore I tell you, whatever you ask for in prayer, believe that you have received it, and it will be yours.**
>
> —MARK 11:24 (NIV)

Though I felt powerless to change anything in this situation, I knew my worries would not help matters either. So, I focused on praying. I felt the briskness of the cool air, breathed in and out, and placed myself in the present—instead of thinking about the past and what we could have done, or the future and what could happen.

I didn't have to feel powerless, knowing I could turn to God. While I couldn't unravel this dilemma myself, God could undo the toughest knots, calming even the most tumultuous sea. In this situation, where I could only pray, I was realizing the need to trust fully in God, putting everything in His hands. Prayer, I was learning more deeply, was the most powerful tool I had.

An eternity seemed to pass as we waited for Dad to return. I wished I could know what was going on. Thankfully, by God's grace, he arrived back home safely. Oddly, it was such a quiet night that there had been no traffic on the road, allowing him to reach the gas station without incident. Fortunately, the gas station was open 24/7, even though most businesses had changed hours due to the pandemic, and the week before, that gas station had been closed.

GOD'S GIFT OF HEARING
— By Tez Brooks —

IN 2018, MISSIONARY Brother James was ministering among previously unreached Tibetan people. He met an old man who was deaf and decided to pray for him. After about ten minutes, the man's hearing came back completely. Brother James then shared the gospel with him. The old man, still in awe over his healing, said, "I wasn't born here. My parents died when I was young, so I was dropped here as a deaf orphan." James explained that God adopts anyone who follows Jesus. The man shouted, "Tell me about this God who healed me. I want to be his adopted child."

My dad had called the police department to help us, but due to fluctuating policies and procedures during the pandemic, they were sending the fire department. That seemed ironic to us since my grandfather who had recently passed away was a firefighter.

Before long, glaring lights flashed across the yard, as the fire truck pulled into the driveway. It seemed almost comical that after our being outside for hours, it took the fire captain mere seconds to replace the remote's battery. The garage door immediately opened. Then, we learned that the name of the captain who had helped us was Chuck. My recently deceased grandfather, who had been a fire captain as well, had been nicknamed Chuck.

I believe there are no coincidences. In following Christ, I have become increasingly attuned to the miraculous ways God works. I've noted how every thread of circumstance in life is impeccably woven together, forming a tapestry that enables us to see God interceding in our lives and giving each stitch meaning.

Being locked out that April night showed me that God sends us special angels to inspire us and connect us to loved ones we've lost. I believe we're never shut out from God—or from those who have left this life for the next. Love isn't severed. Ribbons of connection only grow stronger with these transitions. God is constantly present with us through them all.

At the time I couldn't fathom what purpose the experience of being locked out would serve, but I see now that God made everything fall into place then, just as He still does. God sends His blessings in His mysterious, wonderful ways.

Left Behind in Hiroshima

By Alice J. Wisler

Abandoned. Apparently I'd been left behind on a field trip to the Peace Memorial Museum in Hiroshima. Cold, wet, and jet-lagged, I was left alone to walk the grounds with a small umbrella that leaked droplets onto my shoulders. My suede boots were drenched from stepping into puddles. My coat was not made for a winter's day like this. As the rain pelted me from the gray sky, I wondered how I had fallen into this predicament.

I had been invited to my alma mater, an international high school in Kobe, Japan, to be the alumni-writer-in-residence for a week. I had been born in Japan, a daughter of missionaries, so being back in the country of my childhood was delightful.

That morning had started pleasantly as the twenty-three ninth graders, five chaperones, and I set out on the *Shinkansen* (bullet train) for Hiroshima. Martin, the director of alumni affairs, made sure I had an umbrella since rain was forecast.

During the field trip, we would visit the island of Miyajima, lunch at a local restaurant, shop, then have a chartered bus ride to the Peace Museum. I followed Martin's lead, but I never heard him say what time we were to all meet at the bus after an afternoon inside the museum.

The stories of loss and destruction from the 1945 atomic bomb dropped on Hiroshima were horrific. As I exited the museum, my heart was heavy from seeing artifacts that had belonged to victims and photos of the devastation. But sorrow switched to panic when I noticed the clock on the wall— 3:45 p.m. The train would be leaving soon.

I scanned the gift shop and the snack shop and then rushed outside. *Where were the others?* Plenty of tourists milled around the Peace Memorial Park, but I recognized no one. I scurried toward a side street where the driver had let us off the bus hours earlier. The spot was empty.

Did anyone notice I was not on the bus? Did anyone consider trying to find me?

As I walked from the street over the acreage of wet terrain, pavements, and sod, I didn't know whether I was more ashamed that I wasn't where I was supposed to be or that no one had come to find me.

"Help me, God," I cried when I realized that no amount of walking would get me to a familiar face from our group.

A young blond couple bundled in jackets and scarves walked toward me.

"Excuse me. Do you speak English?" I asked.

"Yes," the woman said, as she and her companion slowed their pace.

"My group left me." I smiled and hoped it sounded warm and not creepy. "Can you believe that?"

"Oh, that's too bad." Her accent was Australian.

"Do you know how to get to the Hiroshima train station?"

"Take the trolley," the man said and pointed to a wide street ahead. "You'll need to get on either number two or six that is headed to the right, not the left."

I repeated the numbers. "How far is the station?"

"Twenty minutes. It's at the end of the line, so you can't miss it."

I thanked the two and walked to the intersection, where I waited for the traffic light to change color so that I could cross to the trolley platform. I tightened my cotton scarf around my neck.

Two men next to me were conversing in Japanese. I stepped closer to them and asked the one in an overcoat if the platform ahead was where I could catch a trolley for Shin-Hiroshima Station. I didn't want to make any more mistakes; I wanted to be sure.

"Yes, it is," he replied in Japanese. "You want either streetcar number two or six."

My time in Japan was short; I hated that this debacle was taking up so much of it. A friend had said to enjoy every moment, and so, as the trolley rumbled along the tracks, I focused on the joy of being back in my birthland and thanked God for the experience of riding a streetcar.

> The LORD will work out his plans for my life—for your faithful love, O LORD, endures forever. Don't abandon me, for you made me.
>
> —PSALM 138:8 (NLT)

I had coins to pay the trolley fare, but I knew I didn't have enough for a train ticket back to Kobe. Martin had my ticket. How would I be able to get back to my hotel room when all I had was a few thousand yen in my purse and the cost of a train ticket was 7,000 yen?

At the station, I asked an employee if there was a cheaper way to make the trek back to Kobe. I also asked if an American man had perhaps left a ticket for me. The answers to both questions were no.

I contemplated what I could do and then I remembered that Pauline, a Canadian friend, lived in the city of Hiroshima. Earlier in the day, we'd chatted via social media, and she'd given me her phone number. Since my cell phone had no service in Japan, I used a public pay phone to call her.

I call upon you, for you will answer me, O God; incline your ear to me; hear my words.

—PSALM 17:6 (ESV)

Pauline said she'd be happy to lend me money for a train ticket and that she'd meet me at the station in half an hour. When she entered the train station, I rushed into her arms. "You are my favorite Canadian," I said.

Pauline smiled. "Let's get you back to Kobe." She took a step, and then paused. "Do you happen to have a credit card?"

I realized that I did have a seldom-used credit card in my purse. "Yes!" I said. I used the card to purchase a ticket. I didn't owe Pauline any money, but I'd always be in her debt for her kindness. She walked with me up the stairs to the platform, watched me board the train and find a seat, and waved goodbye as the train pulled away from the platform.

Seated on the train, I felt both relief and anger. Although grateful for those who had helped me, I was angry with Martin. I could feel it brewing in my heart.

Is this going to be a lesson in forgiveness? I asked God. *Did you bring me ten thousand miles across the ocean to teach me about forgiving? Couldn't you have done that back home in North Carolina?*

Martin offered no apology when we were reunited. He was a punctual man who had no room for those who were late.

When I told him of how I had to rely on others to help me, he said nothing.

Returning to the United States, I unpacked. My boots, a birthday gift my husband had given me years before, were now in sad shape. The heels were torn from my day of wandering in the rain and mud.

The boots could not be repaired, but they sit on the floor of my closet—a reminder of God's provision and presence even in the midst of confusion. That day in Hiroshima, God provided the help I needed from both strangers and friends. God heard my cries as I trudged in the damp and cold. Although my colleague had left me, God never left my side. I always want to be reminded of the way God showers His people with love and compassion, even at our weakest moments.

Walking by faith will cause
all of us to recognize that
as children of God we are
just pilgrims and strangers
down here on this earth.

—J. Vernon McGee, minister

CHAPTER 5

Mysterious Strangers Sent by God

A Light in Winter

By Marilyn Copley Hilton

Christmas was only two weeks away, but I was in no holiday
spirit. Longing to be with my family and friends at home in
California, I'd begun to wonder why I'd accepted the offer to
work in my company's UK office during the coldest part of
the year. I had arrived in early December, and the difference
in the weather couldn't have been starker. The day before I'd
left home, I had strolled with my boyfriend on a sun-drenched
beach in Carmel-by-the-Sea, and now I lived, slept, and worked
under an unending low and bleak sky.

One bright spot was an upcoming visit from a friend from
home, who would stay with me through the holidays. I couldn't
wait to see Joyce's face again, hear her effervescent laughter,
and share cups of tea and the new places I'd discovered. She
would arrive early in the morning, and I'd meet her at Gatwick
Airport.

The evening before her arrival, I left the office and drove
the few miles up the highway to the nearest supermarket to
stock up on essentials and treats for her visit. While I was shopping, a thick fog settled in the area, so thick that while driving
home, I couldn't see more than 3 feet ahead. By this time I'd
adjusted to driving on the left side of the road, but now I had
to deal with this new challenge. Gripping the steering wheel,
I concentrated on keeping my car between the faint lane

markers and within sight of the taillights of the car in front of me. Somehow, I drove those few miles and recognized my exit off the highway and the roads to my flat.

That night I set my alarm for 3:00 a.m., which would give me enough time to dress and drive to Gatwick, and I hoped the fog would be gone by the time I had to leave.

> **The LORD will fight for you, and you have only to be silent.**
>
> —EXODUS 14:14 (ESV)

But when I went out to my car the next morning in the pitch darkness, ice slicked the pavement. As I backed out of the parking space, the ice threatened to send the car sliding down the long driveway and into the street.

There was no way I'd be able to drive anywhere. Joyce would be alone at the airport in an unfamiliar city. I eased my car back into its space.

This was in the days before cell phones, which today would have solved the problem. And I'd also decided not to install a phone in my flat because of the expense and waiting time. Whenever I needed to make a call, I did so from my office in a nearby town—which I couldn't drive to that morning. I had no way of letting Joyce know I would be late in meeting her.

If I could only find a phone nearby, I could call her sister, whom Joyce would certainly call when I wasn't there to meet her. But how and where? Shops weren't open yet. The nearest pay phone was two miles away. I could ask to use a neighbor's phone, but I didn't know anyone in my complex, and I wasn't about to knock on strangers' doors in the middle of the night.

> The LORD is my light
> and my salvation—
> whom shall I fear?
> The LORD is the
> stronghold of my
> life—of whom shall
> I be afraid?
>
> —PSALM 27:1 (NIV)

I got out of my car and searched the dark apartment complex. Except for the streetlamps down on the main road and the stars in the now-clear sky, not a light shone around me.

What could I do? I was out of solutions, and, at that moment, my soul felt as bleak as those English winter skies.

Then, I remembered one more thing—which I should have done from the start. Shivering from cold and close to tears in that dark early morning, I shut my eyes and prayed for help.

"Please, God, I don't know what to do," I said. "Please show me."

When I opened my eyes, a light was glowing in a window at the far end of the complex. Had it been there all along and I'd simply missed it? No, the complex had been completely dark. Would whoever lived there have a phone? I took a step forward, then, doubting my impulse, I halted. What if they didn't open the door? What if they told me to go away? What if they were friendly but didn't have a phone?

But in my doubt, I felt a gentle urging and an inner voice telling me to walk toward that light, with an assurance that all would be well. My favorite scripture verse sprang to mind:

"Have I not commanded you? Be strong and courageous. Do not be afraid; do not be discouraged, for the LORD your God will be with you wherever you go" (Joshua 1:9, NIV).

So, with confidence that those instincts were from God and not my imagination, I obeyed. With my gaze on the light and another prayer in my heart, I walked across the quad to the flat and rang the bell.

The door opened. I was relieved to see a young woman about my age peering through the crack.

"Hello," I said in my gentlest voice, and then explained who I was and why I was at her door at four in the morning.

My words tumbled out. "Do you have a phone and may I use it? I need to call the United States, but will of course charge it to my credit card."

To my great relief, she smiled, opened the door wide, and invited me inside. I stepped into a warm and cozy living room, where another young woman sat on the couch, reading a newspaper.

The two introduced themselves as sisters.

"I'm Ann," said the one who'd opened the door. "This is Rebecca."

"Are you always up this early?" I asked, astonished at the turn of events.

"No," Ann said and laughed. "We're waiting for the stores to open so we can start our Christmas shopping. The best deals are early."

Ann then led me to their phone. I placed the long-distance call to California. After reaching Joyce's sister and explaining the situation, I returned to the living room, feeling lighter than I had since my arrival.

"Will you have some tea?" Rebecca asked.

GOD'S GIFT OF SIGHT

— By Eryn Lynum —

WHILE FOG IS often perceived as an obstruction to a view, it can also bring clarity. With distant horizons shrouded in thick clouds, people can narrow their gaze to what is directly in front of them. Fog focuses attention on the immediate. Perhaps God obscures the future so His children will recognize His present activity. In Matthew 6:34 (NIV), Jesus said, "Therefore do not worry about tomorrow, for tomorrow will worry about itself..." Perhaps the fog rolling in is God's method of removing distractions and focusing His children's hearts on His nearness so that when the fog dissipates, they will confidently follow Him.

The sisters' friendliness and the cheeriness of their home compelled me to linger. And now that I no longer had to be at the airport right away, I gratefully accepted their invitation.

As we sipped our tea Ann asked, "Why are you driving into London? It would be much easier to take the train. And there's a stop at the airport."

The train. I hadn't thought of that, even though I heard its whistle several times a day. And, because the station was only a few blocks from my flat, it would be a short walk.

They told me which train to take and gave me a tip: stay seated until the train reached the end of the line—a few stops past the airport—then get off on the return. It would be easier to navigate to the arrivals area doing this.

I was now doubly thankful for these two sisters—for letting me into their home to use their telephone and for solving my transportation problem. I finished my tea and, warmed by their hospitality and the pale daylight illuminating the eastern sky, I walked with mincing steps on the icy streets to the train station. Within an hour I was united with my friend, who had called her sister and was waiting for me stress-free.

A few days later I carried a poinsettia plant to Ann and Rebecca's flat with a thank-you note for their kindness. No one answered the door, so I left the plant on their doorstep. The next day the poinsettia was still there, and the next. It was on the doorstep the following week, and it was still there in February.

I never again saw light glow in that window or the two sisters who had helped me on that chilly, dark morning. To this day I know they were angels placed there by God, who'd heard my desperate prayer for help and answered in ways I never could have imagined.

Wanda on Assignment

By Therese Marszalek

"What *is* her name, Lord?" I prayed under my breath. Standing in line at the post office in downtown Centralia, Washington, I bobbed to the side to see if I could read the teller's name tag. She wasn't wearing one.

A white-haired and bearded man breezed through the door, waving at the no-tag teller. "Hi, Wanda!" he shouted with a sparkly grin.

Thanks, Lord! I thought to myself. I smiled, clutching three of my most recent books under my arm, a gift I planned to deliver to a stranger I now knew as Wanda. Wanda was a beautiful, fortysomething woman with an inviting smile and friendly countenance.

"Hey, George!" she answered, her smile glistening.

"Next?" the other teller said. Though I was next in line, I motioned for the elderly woman standing behind me to go ahead of me.

"I'm waiting for Wanda," I said, pointing at the other window.

A month earlier, I had lived up to my reputation of being directionally challenged and had ended up in this post office. I had thought I was in the wrong post office in the wrong area. But I soon learned I was at the right post office, just as God planned. In that little post office, He reached out to me through some of the direst needs in my life.

The distress had actually started way before that. When a loved one attempted to take her life, months of dark, tangled trials followed, leaving me feeling completely helpless. Depression and tormenting worry plagued me. The turmoil also took a toll on my marriage and nuclear family. I was weary, drained of all energy physically, emotionally, and spiritually.

As if taking me by the hand, the Lord orchestrated circumstances for me to journey across the state from my home in Spokane to Chehalis, Washington, where I would spend a month with dear friends Doug and Marcia. I embraced this time of rest and refueling, and their beautiful home in the country was like a sanctuary for me to find healing.

> **A generous person will prosper; whoever refreshes others will be refreshed.**
>
> —PROVERBS 11:25 (NIV)

During my second week there, I enjoyed a reflective walk down the windy country road and collected a bountiful harvest of fresh eggs from their chicken coop. Then Marcia and I sat on the back deck as she told me about her hectic day as a mechanical engineer. Suddenly I broke out in a profuse sweat, became dizzy, and lost consciousness as my chin dropped to my chest.

Doug and Marcia insisted that I get medical attention, but because I had little memory of the episode, I hesitated.

"I'm fine," I tried to assure them. "It was probably just from taking a long walk in the heat."

Yet after two days of worrying that I'd had a minor stroke or seizure, I agreed to go to the emergency room. That hospital visit led to a battery of diagnostic tests, doctors, and appoint-ments. I had to rely on my friends to transport me. In the end, all tests were inconclusive, leaving me with no answers and over $9,000 of unexpected medical costs.

> **Carry each other's burdens, and in this way you will fulfill the law of Christ.**
>
> —GALATIANS 6:2 (NIV)

When I was cleared to drive, I hopped into my cherry-red Sebring to mail some packages that were now overdue for shipping. I took a wrong turn and ended up following my GPS to find the nearest post office.

A parking spot awaited me in front of the tiny post office nestled in downtown Centralia. A long line also awaited me inside. Feeling my physi-cal and emotional weariness, I became lost in thought.

"Ma'am? May I help you?" the teller said, snapping me out of my introspection.

"I need to ship these," I said, stepping to the window. Wanda's warm eyes welcomed me, and her kind smile warmed my heart. Taking my packages, she kept smiling, staring into my eyes longer than was comfortable, almost as if she was study-ing me. As she rattled off my shipping options, I answered her questions, and then slid her my credit card.

"Thank you, Therese," she said, taking a second look at my card. "You have a nice day, now!" As she handed me the credit card and receipt, her smile seemed to hug me goodbye. Amid my health concerns, my grief over the family distress, and the general uneasiness of life, her kindness was more than a passing pleasantry. In some odd way, it filled me with the warmth of a presence that went beyond this human form. This stranger seemed like a heavenly ambassador, embodying and emanating the love of God Himself. The glow of God's presence stayed with me for days, bolstering me in some unexplainable way.

Now, as I stepped up to Wanda's window a month later, her smile greeted me again. "May I help you?"

My eyes watered. Sudden emotion made words stick in my throat. Wanda reached out her hand as if to comfort me. "I was here a month ago and you waited on me," I told her. "I was going through some very painful circumstances."

I briefly told Wanda what had happened.

"Do you ever wonder if you're making a difference?" I asked. She nodded with questioning eyes. "God used you to touch my life in a powerful way that day."

Wanda began to cry. "These are for you," I said, pushing the personally inscribed books toward her. "I want to bless you with some of my books. You're an angel in disguise."

Wiping her tears, she said, "Can I hug you?"

"Of course!" I said. Wanda left her post and reappeared in the lobby through the swinging door. We embraced as the other customers watched. No words were necessary.

As I stepped back into my car, the skies opened, and the black cloud above dumped pounding rain that only lasted a few minutes. As I drove back to my country sanctuary, the sun reappeared, and a colorful rainbow arched across the sky.

Life's storms will come again, I sensed God whisper in my heart. *But I will always be with you.*

Remembering the rainbow God used in Noah's time as a sign that He would never again flood the earth, I smiled, knowing that God had sent Wanda to me as a sign:

And God said, "This is the sign of the covenant I am making between me and you and every living creature with you, a covenant for all generations to come: I have set my rainbow in the clouds, and it will be the sign of the covenant between me and the earth. Whenever I bring clouds over the earth and the rainbow appears in the clouds, I will remember my covenant between me and you and all living creatures of every kind. Never again will the waters become a flood to destroy all life. Whenever the rainbow appears in the clouds, I will see it and remember the everlasting covenant between God and all living creatures of every kind on the earth." (Genesis 9:12–15, NIV)

"Thank You, Lord, for sending the rainbow. Thank You for sending Wanda," I said.

I may never see Wanda again, but I will always think of her as an angel on assignment who brought me loving comfort in a dire time of need, a welcome sign to remind me that God is always near.

My Mysterious Lumberjack

By Annettee Budzban

My old oak tree was managing to remain standing in spite of its bald spots from the weathered and worn bark. But since I was living on a tight budget as a single mother with two young boys, I couldn't afford to have it cut down. Besides, it was one of my favorite shade trees.

One night while I was lying in bed, I was startled awake by a crash of thunder. Between each new *boom*, the wind howled, and I heard the tree branches wrestling. As the wind continued to blow fiercely, I heard my beloved old oak tree creaking.

"I just can't lose that tree. And please keep my boys safe from harm," I prayed.

The next morning, I jumped out of bed and went to the boys' room. I opened their blinds.

"Oh no!" I gasped. The mighty old oak was split in pieces!

I noted that the trunk was intact. However, half of the tree was lying in my yard, surrounded by broken limbs and shattered bark. The other half had landed on the cyclone fence, leaving a rather large dent and mangled-up chain-link fencing. Large branches and other debris were strewn across the top of my neighbor's garage. My heart sank at the sight of the damage.

I realized why I had felt the urgency to pray for protection over the boys' room during this storm. If those branches had landed on my roof instead of my neighbor's garage, they could have landed on the roof over the boys' room. *Thank You, God, for keeping the boys safe,* I silently prayed.

> **Do not forget to show hospitality to strangers, for by so doing some people have shown hospitality to angels without knowing it.**
>
> —HEBREWS 13:2 (NIV)

As I scanned the destruction left behind, I was perplexed by what to do about the situation. The tree problem was more than I was physically or emotionally able to cope with. I really needed some help.

I gazed out the window and asked God, "Please send someone to help with this tree."

I couldn't concentrate at work that day, so I took the afternoon off to start my quest to remove the mess. Not sure where to begin, I did a Google search to find someone who could cut down the tree and remove the debris. I pleaded with each person I called. "That large storm we had last night broke my oak tree in half. And part of the tree is on the roof of my neighbor's garage! Can you help?"

My quest for help waned when I was quoted $350 to cut down the tree. That didn't include the removal of the tree remains from my yard—that would cost another $200 or more! As I felt that sinking feeling again, I prayed, "Lord, I need help. There is no way I can come up with this much money."

I knew I had to place my predicament in God's hands. Amazingly my neighbor was gracious and wasn't pressing me about the branch removal.

After three days of my frantically searching and praying for an answer, a friend came by after work. She invited me out for some coffee and dessert...her treat! She knew how troubling and exhausting the tree problem had become for me and wanted to relieve my worries, if only for a little while.

We sat in the corner booth at the restaurant, eating cake and laughing. I could feel the frustration fade away with every chuckle. And I felt every delicious bite of rich chocolate cake soothe my senses.

When we returned to my house, my friend pulled over to the curb to drop me off. We lingered in the car a while longer, laughing as we savored the moment. However, our laughter ceased as a man reeled around the corner on his bicycle. He appeared carefree, his check-ered, flannel shirt flapping in the breeze. My friend and I exchanged a perplexed look as this man coasted right past us into my driveway, dismounted his bike, and approached my front porch. I briskly walked to the porch to see what his visit was about.

> **You are my hiding place; you will deliver me from trouble.**
>
> —PSALM 32:7 (ISV)

"Hi," he said with a bright smile and steely blue eyes penetrating into mine. "My name is Jack. I was riding my bike through your neighborhood and noticed you have a tree that needs to be cut down."

GOD'S GIFT OF HEARING
— By Lawrence W. Wilson —

IN MARCH 2015, Lynn Jennifer Groesbeck lost control of her car and landed in Utah's Spanish Fork River. A fisherman spotted the car the next morning and called police. By the time first responders arrived, fourteen hours had passed since the accident. According to NBC News, three firefighters and two police officers waded into the river drawn by an adult voice calling, "Help me, help me." Yet Groesbeck was found dead in the car, believed to have died on impact. However, her eighteen-month-old daughter, Lily, miraculously survived, hanging upside down in her car seat, just above the icy water.

I was all ears. He said, "I could cut it down and remove all the debris for sixty-five dollars."

I was stunned! I paused for a moment, thinking how this bargain seemed too good to be true. However, I didn't have the money until I got paid on Friday, so it wouldn't do much good. I said, "I won't have the money until Friday; could you return then?"

"No problem," he replied. "I'll come by tomorrow, cut down the tree, haul it away, and come back on Friday to collect my pay."

His offer was amazing! I quickly responded, "That would be great!"

The next day when I arrived home from work, I observed several small pieces of tree bark scattered on the driveway. I ran to the backyard and noticed sunlight streaming down into my backyard on the spot my oak tree had once shaded. True to his word, Jack had cut down the tree and removed all the branches.

When Friday rolled around, Jack came by and picked up his money. As he walked to the end of the driveway, I waved goodbye. I stood there watching until he faded into the distance. I never saw him again. Then it hit me! *Hmmm, his name was Jack, and he wore a red-and-black-checkered flannel shirt resembling that of a lumberjack. Who was this mysterious lumberjack? Could he be an angel sent from above?*

I wasn't sure where God dispensed him from. But God was true to His word to send a mysterious lumberjack to help in my time of need. Although I know God is present at all times and in all places, I got a firsthand look at how He assigns His angels as servants and messengers to do His bidding.

Help out of the Blue

By Rhonda Dragomir

"I'm going to talk to my people." Dale, my half-Romanian, American-born husband grinned impishly and exited our car for a romp into the great unknown. The line of vehicles waiting to cross the border from Hungary into Romania snaked for more than two miles. The overthrow of communism in 1989, only six months before our visit, had wreaked chaos. We were about to enter the fray.

"You don't speak Romanian," I called, but my pointing out the obvious didn't faze Dale. His excitement about meeting people from the land of his grandfather trumped any linguistic challenges.

Dacias—compact cars driven by most Romanians—sat parked on a two-lane road where they sweltered in the mid-summer sun. To escape the heat, people had shut off their engines, exited their cars, and leaned against them, whiling away the time in conversation. They didn't expect to move anytime soon.

Dale approached a cluster of men who appraised him with curiosity. Our bright-red German Volkswagen Golf stood out like an apple in a basket of snowballs. After a brief interaction, the Romanians waved their arms and pointed ahead. Though their words sounded like gibberish to us, their gestures spoke volumes. They wanted us to go to the front of the line.

When he joined me again, Dale said there was a separate, much shorter line for foreigners. But there were only two lanes, and, occasionally, a vehicle traveled the opposite way. I opposed the idea, but my intrepid husband would not be deterred. Dale revved the engine and swung into the passing lane. I was married to a madman.

My fingernails left an impression in the armrest. Eventually, the towers of the crossing gatehouse loomed ahead. God's answer to my prayers came in the form of Hungarian guards who slowed traffic the other way.

Only two or three vehicles were ahead of us in the line for foreigners, but uniformed soldiers with machine guns blocked our way. They waved us off, clearly wanting us to return to the end of the line we'd just left. Dale decided not to argue with the armed men. He executed a perfect three-point turn, and we went back to our original position.

After parking the car and killing the engine, Dale again approached the same group of men. Their agitation grew with every word. Dale threw up his hands in a what-else-can-I-do gesture. The commotion drew others out of their cars. Where I saw a potentially violent mob, Dale reveled in their support. The speed and volume of their words increased, and my unease escalated into panic.

Several vehicles passed us, ignoring the danger as Dale had done. Most were German or Hungarian. None returned. That cemented Dale's decision to try again. He took the wheel like Mad Max driving a fuel tanker. We'd make a second attempt, but I envisioned us sitting in the Romanian hoosegow.

Dale passed car after car and didn't stop until he was only a foot behind a blue Volkswagen van with German license plates. He fixed his eyes straight ahead and refused to look at the soldiers, whose shouts could not be mistaken for "Welcome to Romania."

"Look," Dale said, pointing at the rear window of the van. "It's a sign." Weathered, ragged, and stained, the bumper sticker contained only a symbol—the ichthus fish. It did not have the Greek letters, but there was no mistaking the universal emblem of Christian fellowship since the second century.

Ignoring the soldiers, Dale again exited our car against my advice. He approached the blue van and knocked on the window. This time, the conversation lasted many excruciating minutes. I could have joined in if I'd had enough courage, but our car was my safe place.

When Dale returned, I grabbed his arm and demanded, "What did you say?"

He leaned his head back and said a prayer of thanks. When he noticed that the present strain might cause me to rupture an important internal organ, he said, "They rolled down the window, and I asked, 'Does anybody here speak English?'"

They did. And their advice sent tingles to all my extremities.

With the collapse of central oversight, most Romanian governmental, military, and civil institutions became fiefdoms. Greedy people, long oppressed financially and philosophically, saw no wrong in profiting from their positions. Border guards were apparently among the worst, making their own policies and enforcing them capriciously. It was somewhat equivalent to the Wild West in America in the 1890s.

When the Germans asked the purpose of our visit, Dale had been completely forthright. He told them of our quest to adopt one of the many orphans we'd read about in the news. With no effective social welfare system in Romania, orphanages over-flowed with babies and toddlers from poverty-stricken homes.

The flood of Westerners to adopt these children created a boon for border guards. They often extorted unsuspecting visitors, demanding they exchange all their currency at the official rate, or they would be denied entrance. This decreased the value of a traveler's funds by almost two-thirds. When the guards traded Western currency with street vendors, they enjoyed unbelievable profits.

We carried only $10,000 in cash.

I yielded to the tremors that fought to gain control of my body. What would we do? Our American Romanian friends had advised us how much money to bring to secure the adoption. A devaluation like this would turn our dream into a nightmare.

One of our new German friends had asked Dale if we could provide any humanitarian aid. Before we had left home for Romania, we had learned the horrific news that AIDS was rampant in the orphanages from the reuse of dirty needles. To help, we had bought syringes in bulk before we left America. They were tucked in our suitcases, along with diapers, formula, and baby clothing. When we mentioned this, our helpers advised us to state the purpose of our visit as humanitarian and not to mention adoption.

> This is what the LORD says: "In the time of my favor I will answer you, and in the day of salvation I will help you."
>
> —ISAIAH 49:8 (NIV)

We agreed and filled out the paperwork accordingly. But if the guards opened our luggage, they would know immediately what we planned to do in Romania.

The wait seemed interminable. We prayed and watched as the swarm of soldiers moved from vehicle to vehicle like bees in a field of clover. They reached the blue van, and its three occupants emerged wearing broad smiles. Parcels exchanged hands, accompanied by nodding and backslapping.

> Do not be anxious about anything, but in every situation, by prayer and petition, with thanksgiving, present your requests to God.
>
> —PHILIPPIANS 4:6 (NIV)

I fought a chill despite the heat. We prayed out loud, pleading with God to help us find favor with the soldiers. When our friends got back in their van and pulled away, our time had come. For better or worse, we would face the guards and learn our fate.

A burly man waved us forward, one of the same ones who had previously turned us back. Dale pulled to a stop and turned over our entrance papers. After perusing them, the guard pointed to a suitcase and said, "You open." He had chosen the very one with the baby items, but it also contained the syringes and my flute, which I had brought to play in church services. He raised an eyebrow, and I lifted my hands to playing position and wiggled my fingers. Somehow, I managed a weak smile despite my terror.

Soon enough the guard nodded his head and pointed toward the gate. "You go."

We eased across the border and pulled into a small parking lot where the blue van had stopped, waiting for us.

Hugs and introductions came first and then the explanation. These men had smuggled Bibles into Romania for years. They were well-known by the guards for being generous with their "gifts," and the customary rules were skirted at their discretion.

That day, after they finished their schmooze session with the guards, our new friends had pointed at our little red car. "See them?" they had said. "They're with us."

Gratitude for God's impeccable timing washed over us. Our first attempt to cross the border, if successful, would have ended in disaster. But our returning to the back of the line allowed time for God's favor to go before us. Even in my great anxiety, He guided us every step of the way.

Our time of favor came three weeks into our quest. Having been told there were no babies available for adoption in any of the five orphanages we visited, we acted on the scriptural admonition in James 4:2 (NIV): "You do not have because you do not ask God." We asked. Very specifically, we prayed for a little girl with brown eyes and hair. And just for fun, we asked that she look a little like each of us.

Nine days later God led us to our child not in an orphanage, but in a private home where a family sacrificed much to protect her from neglect and disease. When we first saw her, amazement and joy merged in a lightning strike of answered prayer. Her cherubic face framed with a cap of wispy brown hair, her wide eyes as chocolate Hershey kisses—she was a carbon copy of my brother as a baby. We named her Jana, Slavic for "God is gracious." She was perfect.

Three grueling and amazing weeks later, we passed through the same gate in the other direction. I drove while Dale walked across at his insistence, like Moses on the path God made through the Red Sea. He cradled our four-month-old daughter, brought to us in God's perfect time and assisted—at least in part—by men and angels on wings of a blue Volkswagen.

To be fully seen by somebody, then, and to be loved anyhow—this is a human offering that can border on the miraculous.

—Elizabeth Gilbert, author

CHAPTER 6

Life-Changing Relationships

Dogs and Moose and Bears, Oh My!

By Mary Kay Moody

No matter how far we travel, we're never out of God's sight or His reach. One summer He used a chickenhearted dog to remind me of this truth.

From the time my son Karl was knee-high, he wanted adventure. He sought out high places at the playground and relished a scramble up Old Rag, a peak in the Blue Ridge Mountains. Once I couldn't find him in our apartment, and his buddy's mom couldn't find either of them in hers. We went outside and were hailed by the two four-year-olds sitting on the roof of the back porch—three stories up!

In addition to heights, Karl always loved animals and wanted a dog more than almost anything. This, however, was not negotiable for a mom with major allergies.

I shouldn't have been surprised when he announced he intended to be Grizzly Adams when he grew up. Our preteen mountain-man-wannabe celebrated when we moved to a house on the edge of the woods and he could get an outside dog—a Husky.

Having a dog didn't diminish Karl's desire to walk off into the woods someday to live a hermit's life. When he was about fifteen, I teased him that he enjoyed television too much to do that. He assured me wilderness beat out TV. He asked if I'd be OK with saying goodbye when he was older, not knowing if or when I'd see him again. Whew!

But knowing his mother's heart, he suggested a compromise, offering to schedule a reunion every five years or so, reminding me that he'd be without calendar or watch so timing would have to be approximate.

I was beginning to think he might not grow out of this desire. He'd held it fiercely for ten years. He read towers of books on camping and surviving various weather conditions, He pored over Boy Scout manuals and camped in our yard and in nearby woods. He practiced more survival skills than I could count. He was equipped.

> ## The LORD is good, a strong refuge when trouble comes.
>
> —NAHUM 1:7 (NLT)

We figured if he planned to walk into the mountains someday, we'd better ensure he had a taste of it. So for his sixteenth birthday, we gave him a trip to a three-week wilderness camp in California's High Sierras. He returned more determined than ever.

After high-school graduation, Karl became a cook at a local restaurant. One afternoon a regular customer stopped by our home. She worked at an animal shelter, and they had a dog that was about to be put down. It was so afraid of people that nobody would adopt it. She asked Karl to take it. His beloved Husky had recently died, and he said he wasn't ready for another. But the woman lifted out of her car a medium-sized black dog with brown-tipped ears. It slid backward under the car, so terrified that Karl suspected it'd been beaten. He sat and coaxed the dog out. Soon it was in his lap, and the two were inseparable. He named her Echo.

> **For the angel of the LORD is a guard; he surrounds and defends all who fear him.**
>
> —PSALM 34:7 (NLT)

Although Echo bonded with Karl, she remained terrified of everyone else. When my husband, Ed, or I left the house, Echo ran into the farthest corner of her doghouse and trembled. When she was fed, she picked up one piece of kibble, retreated inside the doghouse to eat, then ventured forth and repeated until she emptied the bowl. Watching her be so frightened was painful. Six months passed before she ate normally.

A number of commitments slowed Karl's departure, but in spring when he was twenty-one he planned another foray into the wilderness, with an eye toward deciding where he'd launch his dream for good. This time he was headed to Alaska.

As a mom, I always felt better knowing where my kids were. If I'd ever been there, all the better because I could visualize it. Karl, on the other hand, was nonchalant. He figured he'd done his part by being prepared, and God would do whatever He chose to do. So Karl took off on a plane and disappeared from my vision. Thankfully he didn't disappear from God's vision.

We had waved him off in early May, Echo in tow. In mid-May we headed off on our own adventure—driving the Pacific Coast from San Diego to Seattle. I didn't like being away while Karl was, but we were locked into our reservations. We prayed (it felt like constantly!) for him to be safe on his wide-open adventure. Being a parent to such a child is challenging. You learn early on to not let fear control you. Still, having him fly into wilderness with a dog, a pack, and not much money was disquieting.

Karl called on day three to let us know he'd connected with a sorority sister of mine who lived in Anchorage. He stayed with her for a few days until he landed a job at a lodge near the Matanuska Glacier and River. Because he worked four long days per week and had three off, he got in a lot of hiking and camping. It all sounded great, and as we traveled, I imagined him performing his chef duties while Echo waited in his room, then hiking through cool, pristine forests with a roaring river to one side and a blue-white glacier ahead.

He connected with us only twice as we traveled, enthusiastically reporting his hikes and rambles on the glacier. He casually mentioned he'd seen a moose. Equally casually he related how one night while they camped, Echo woke him with a persistent, low growl while she remained lying near him. In the twilight, a black bear pawed through his firepit, searching for food. Finding none, it soon lumbered into the woods.

The truth about these sanitized stories wouldn't be revealed until four months later when Karl came home. The truth is, Karl experienced the black bear incident just two days into his first camping trip. The 250-pound animal was only 30 feet from where Karl slept. When telling us the story, he comforted me with the facts that he'd seen only one other black bear, and on later camping trips he slept 100 feet away from where he cooked. Still, it didn't seem far enough!

"Seeing the moose" was only the first step in that escapade. It was standing in the river. Karl, in the forest, was perhaps 100 yards from the thousand-pound creature. He dropped his pack and retrieved his camera. When he looked through the viewfinder, the moose was stepping over the 5-foot-high riverbank as easily as you'd step over a curb. Then she charged.

Echo, barking fiercely, shot to one side about 30 feet away. The moose slowed, eyeing Karl, then the dog, apparently trying to decide which to attack first. Then Karl noticed the moose's calf still in the river. The moose made her decision and headed toward Karl.

Everything happened quickly. Karl had noticed a ring of three trees close together, and he stepped into the center. Echo, barking, charged the moose and as she circled the trees trying to reach Karl, Echo followed, snapping at her lower legs. She continued circling for what Karl said was probably a minute but felt like an hour. But when she realized Echo stood between her and her calf, the moose gave up and returned to her baby.

We didn't learn until later that there was yet a third time the dog performed such a feat. One sunny day Karl and a coworker were hiking with their three dogs. As they walked along a path, suddenly the dogs barked like crazy, ran 20 to 30 feet ahead, returned, and repeated the circuit—constantly.

Karl assumed the dogs spotted a deer and wondered why they didn't go into the woods after it—until ahead, in the middle of the trail, they discovered a pile of bear scat. A very big pile, still giving off heat. They'd walked on a short way when they smelled the rank odor of a grizzly bear.

They turned and walked down to the river, the dogs reluctantly following. The two men knew if they went into the water, the cold and rocks would be their death. But at least walking along the river, they only had to watch one direction. As they walked, they planned.

Suddenly Karl realized they'd given the bear an invitation to stalk and attack them because they'd each put a frozen steak

GOD'S GIFT OF SMELL
— By Lawrence W. Wilson —

TECHNICALLY, NO ONE has ever been able to smell what's outside a space vehicle. There is no atmosphere in space, and no air pressure, so it would be fatal for an astronaut to remove the helmet. Yet several space walkers have encountered a unique scent at the moment after removing their helmet in the space shuttle airlock. Others have said they detected the scent on fabric suits that had been worn in space. One astronaut compared it to "pleasant, sweet smelling welding fumes." Though space is mostly a vacuum, there are some molecules present. Apparently, it has its own scent.

---

in their backpacks that morning. By now the steaks had thawed somewhat and were enticing the bear ever closer.

Noticing a spit of rocks jutting into the river, they stopped on the rocky promontory, built a fire, cooked, and ate the steaks, leaving some meat and the bones in a pile for the bear. They walked off hoping their offering would satisfy the grizzly. Apparently the idea worked because before long, the dogs quit their frenetic chasing and incessant barking, and they didn't see the bear. They hiked a good distance before setting up camp with no more overwrought dogs or eau-de-grizzly.

These stories, though harrowing to hear, remind me that while our son was separated from us, he wasn't separated from God. I know that the dog that huddled under the car that day turned out to be not only an angel in fur, but also an echo of God's presence and grace.

A Beautiful Journey Home

By Del Bates

"Are you the new nail technician here?" This classy lady had an oversized black leather bag and a smile to warm anyone's heart.

"Yes, I am," I said. "Would you like a manicure?"

Those words with Jan, thirty-plus years ago, were the onset of one of the closest friendships in my life.

Jan became a regular client and, for some reason, continued to follow me from salon to salon, even if I didn't tell her where I was going. When she came in, she never rattled on about God or her strong faith, but she had something I wanted, although I didn't know what it was.

I mean, who would ask me to lunch and then hijack me in her car afterward and ask me if I wanted to pray?

"For what?" I'd reply. "It's not Sunday; why would we pray now?"

Finally, after more lunches together, she introduced me to Jesus and my life took a drastic turn. Our friendship grew to a new dimension. Our days were centered around prayer, praise, and worship as I embarked on a relationship with this God I'd never known personally until now. And prayer was our common thread that bonded us to Him.

As the years passed, sad to say, so did Jan's memory. Then she was diagnosed with Alzheimer's. The Jan I knew was different, yet the same. The sweet spirit of the Lord that dwelt within never left her.

Though we could not do things we enjoyed before, nothing stopped us from chatting over a two- or three-hour lunch. Sometimes, as patients with Alzheimer's do, she'd repeat the same things over and over. But I listened and laughed or cried as if hearing what she said for the first time.

Since I was unfamiliar with this disease, I had no idea how the end would come. All I know is when I stopped in to see Jan, who lived with her daughter, Kristen, and she asked Jan, "Mom, do you know who this is?" Jan put her hands together as if to pray and said, "I sure do."

One who has unreliable friends soon comes to ruin, but there is a friend who sticks closer than a brother.

—PROVERBS 18:24 (NIV)

Oh, the warmth in my soul as she opened her arms to welcome me with a precious "Jan" hug.

Then I got the call. "Jan's gone down suddenly. She's lost all mobility, and it could be any day now for her to go home to be with the Lord."

As I entered Kristen's home, I was unprepared for what lay ahead. The glory of God greeted me at the door. I dropped my purse and grabbed hold of Kristen's arm. "Oh, my goodness! The glory! The presence is so strong here. What is going on? What is happening?"

"Oh, Mom Del"—as Kristen referred to me—"it's God. He's here!"

And He was—along with every angel assigned to Jan for such a time as this. For the next few days, her loved ones sat at her bedside listening to peaceful songs of worship as the presence of God continued to fill the room.

Each of us continued to share "Jan" stories we held dear to our hearts. Time continued to pass, and we thought each breath would be Jan's last. We gently rubbed her face and hands, commenting that her skin was as soft as a newborn child. We laughed, cried, and questioned how close she was from here to eternity.

Rejoice evermore. Pray without ceasing.

—1 THESSALONIANS 5:16–17 (KJV)

I even whispered in her ear, "Jan, tell me what it's like. What do you see? Is it as glorious as we always heard it would be?"

Silent tears warmed my heart as her daughters and each person who surrounded her bed talked about how much they loved her. Then, one by one, they gave her permission to leave, knowing it was her time to go.

The night passed, and the sun rose one more time. A gal from hospice stopped by to sit with Jan and her daughters. She strummed on her guitar and sang one of the songs dear to Jan's heart, "What a Beautiful Name." The presence of God filled the room along with angels to aid Jan in her final journey home. As the hospice worker sang the words ever so softly, Jan's spirit gracefully left her body and was released to her eternal home.

Tears dampened the crisp sheets that lay upon her lifeless body. Hearts broke as the sting of grief filled the air. Yet, for the first time, I experienced the beauty of death. Jan's spirit was set free from this bondage called life and released into the glorious light of eternity.

Scripture tells us unless a kernel of wheat falls to the ground and dies, it remains only a single seed. But if it dies, it produces many seeds: It cannot live again (John 12:24).

We know that death was just the beginning with Jan. And for those left behind, it's time to pick up the baton and carry Jan's legacy to all the generations to come.

I will miss her dearly. God's presence was there from the first time she asked for a manicure. But the love of God she imparted to me is something I will share with all.

As Jan crossed over the threshold of life, I believe she was welcomed with the words she always wanted to hear: "Well done, thou good and faithful servant" (Matthew 25:21, KJV).

Clothesline Legacy

By Elizabeth W. Peterson

Raising both hands high above her head to throw the corner of a wet sheet over the clothesline, my not-quite-5-foot mother then stooped down to take a wooden pin from my small hand. Since I was not old enough to start school, I was at home to help with routine housework.

Shouldering the bag of clothespins, I walked with her up and down the clothesline as she sang all four verses of hymns. I didn't know it then, but during those moments at the clothesline, she was passing down a legacy of how she experienced God's presence while she was working.

As she moved from one row of wash to another, she used her routine to sing hymns of praise to affirm her strong faith in God. On days when she appeared tired or discouraged, her list of praise hymns grew lengthier, and she sang with more expression, as though she were praying for strength.

Armed with words from her favorite hymns, she lifted the basket piled high with a mound of wet clothes and moved up and down the steel lines strung between wooden posts, until it was empty. My feet skipped to mark the tempo of Fanny Crosby's hymn "To God Be the Glory," or Martin Luther's "A Mighty Fortress Is Our God." With each row of sheets hung, she would start another stanza of the same song.

While we worked together to empty the basket of wet clothes, on most mornings, flocks of birds flew down and lined up on a telephone wire, as if they wanted to be part of the backyard choir.

Whenever the serenading of the birds grew too loud to ignore, my mother looked up and sometimes clapped her hands to thank the heavenly choir for offering praise to their heavenly Father. I could understand the birds serenading God on those bright sunny mornings, but how could my mother find anything in our lives to praise God about? Life in our family during the post-war period was not easy.

> **Tell your children about it, let your children tell their children, and their children another generation.**
>
> —JOEL 1:3 (NKJV)

Just putting food on our table was a struggle for our mother. My father brought his weekly earnings home at the end of the week, and I would see my parents stuffing cash into budget envelopes they kept inside an empty oatmeal box. At our morning breakfast table, Mama faithfully prayed that God would send customers to Daddy's barbershop for a haircut or a morning shave to provide money to pay the family's bills.

In the winter I walked beside her as she carried a metal bucket to the coal bin in our garage and filled it to bring into the house to heat our four-room duplex. I could see the cold winter air being dappled with her warm breath as she continued her symphony of praise. Her insurmountable faith astounded me.

I wondered what she could find in her life to sing about. Even a preschool child could see that God had forgotten this family of six, crowded into a four-room home with only a stove to keep us warm in the winter and a few window fans to cool us in the South Carolina summer.

> **You shall teach them to your children, speaking of them when you sit in your house, when you walk by the way, when you lie down, and when you rise up.**
>
> —DEUTERONOMY 11:19 (NKJV)

One day, I recall looking at her lined face as she bent over the clothes basket. I blurted out the question I had wanted to ask for far too long, "Why do you keep singing? You do not have anything in your life to make you happy!" And I began to list the hardships she faced, as I leaned against her small frame.

My question seemed to surprise her. She dropped the basket to cradle me in her arms and say, "Oh, honey, I am not worried. I have the Lord." It was hard not to think of all she did not have so I determined she must not see all the difficulties our family faced.

Didn't she see there was never enough money and no car to take us to the places we needed to go? Or was she pretending that those hardships were not there? I saw nothing in our life to make her happy or offer praises to God.

Her example of being in God's presence was not limited to singing hymns. I saw it when she helped me memorize Scripture verses before I learned to read. I would stand beside

GOD'S GIFT OF HEARING
— By Lawrence W. Wilson —

SPOKEN WORDS ARE processed primarily by the superior temporal lobes of the brain. However, music is processed in many parts of the brain, including those that govern movement, pulse, mood, and memory. That's why an Alzheimer's patient may sing along to a familiar tune yet no longer recognize close relatives. Some sounds unlock knowledge hidden deep in the mind, and not all "speech" uses words. As the psalmist said, "The heavens declare the glory of God... They have no speech, they use no words; no sound is heard from them. Yet their voice goes out into all the earth" (Psalm 19:1–4, NIV).

---

her at the ironing board or when she was washing dishes and recite phrases of a verse until I could say the entire scripture.

Each morning she would come into my room, open the blinds to wake me up, and ask me to pray our morning verse to God. "My voice shalt thou hear in the morning, O LORD: in the morning will I direct my prayer unto thee, and will look up" (Psalm 5:3, KJV). We would end with "Amen."

Each evening before going to sleep, she would come to kneel with me beside my bed and we would pray together our nighttime verse, "I will both lay me down in peace, and sleep: for thou, LORD, only makes me dwell in safety" (Psalm 4:8, KJV).

Decades later I told the story of the clothesline legacy to my mother as she lay in the Alzheimer's unit of a nursing home. Her eyes sparkled and she smiled while I shared the story of a mother who sang beautiful hymns as she hung out the wash with her little daughter who asked how she could still sing even though her life was hard.

Her disease had erased the memory of who was sitting beside her bed, but her lips moved to form some of the words I sang from the old hymnal I kept beside her bed.

Years after my mother passed away, my daughter now asks similar questions as she watches me struggle to live confined to a wheelchair after years of paralysis due to multiple sclerosis. "I don't know how you do it, Mom," she says as she helps me dress or fix my hair.

"Oh, honey..." I say and pause to picture my mother saying similar words to me before I pass on the truth handed down to me, with faith that my daughter will pass it on to her children.

After the Wreck

By Marcia Gunnett Woodard

"There's been a terrible accident. Your dad didn't make it, and if you want to see your mom, you need to hurry."

When I got off the phone, all I could do was sit on the living room floor, sobbing and begging God not to let me be an orphan. The loss of the love, support, and guidance of my dad seemed a burden of grief too heavy to bear, even without the loss of my mom.

We threw a few things in a suitcase and pushed the speed limit as we drove three hours to the city where Mom had been transported by emergency medical helicopter. We arrived at the hospital as the dusk of a dull, gray evening settled down over the city. There wasn't even a dusting of snow, which made driving easier, but did nothing to relieve our ominous foreboding.

Making matters worse, the hospital was in the midst of remodeling, with hallways blocked off, plastic sheeting covering doors, and directional signs that had been removed from the walls and were now lying on the floor, pointing at nothing.

The hospital offices were closed for the night, so no one was around who could help us find the critical-care unit. In fact, there seemed to be nobody at all in the wing of the hospital we entered. We seemed to be all alone.

Then, in the distance, I heard a woman's voice giving directions to someone.

"OK, now we turn left here, then we follow this wall down to the second doorway on the right."

Her voice was distinctive—unlike any I'd ever heard before, unfamiliar, yet somehow comforting. As we followed the maze created by draped sheets of plastic, she continued to talk, and her voice came closer and closer.

Suddenly, a hand swept aside the plastic sheeting, and a couple stepped into our "maze." The woman was tiny, with curly dark hair and glasses, and she smiled a greeting. The man was tall and slim, with a pleasant face, but he had a blank look in his eyes. In one hand, he held a folded white cane, while his other hand rested on the woman's shoulder. In an instant, I knew them!

"Are you Pam and Tony?"

These were Mom's good friends from church. Mom had told me stories about Pam and Tony, who didn't let vision problems stop him—but I had never met them. Now, here they were, facing me—I was sure of it!

The woman's smile got even bigger.

"Yes, we are! And you must be Marcia. We've heard so much about you! We were on our way home from vacation, and we had stopped to see our daughter and her family. She lives here in the suburbs, you know. Anyway, we got the news about your parents, and we knew that God had us so close to the hospital for a reason. So, we came over here to stay with your mom until you folks could get here. Come on! I'll show you where the elevator is to critical care."

When we got to critical care, Mom had just come out of surgery, and it looked like there was a chance that she might make it. Fortunately, she did survive that night, and began an amazing five months of transition from trauma bay to critical care to rehab, and finally home.

It was one of the loneliest times of my life, as I stayed behind at the hospital with Mom. I supported her as she learned to navigate the world without her lifelong love, while at the same time I dealt with my grief over the death of my dad. And I longed to be at home to comfort my kids as they mourned the loss of their grandad.

> **All praise to God, the Father of our Lord Jesus Christ. God is our merciful Father and the source of all comfort.**
>
> —2 CORINTHIANS 1:3 (NLT)

Usually, it was the little things, like registering Mom as a hospital patient, that got me. I had never really thought about the question, "Marital status?" before. But as I came to that space on the form, it hit me like a punch in the gut, and as I marked the box labeled "widowed" I wept, not caring who saw.

But in spite of the times of loneliness and grief, we met many people along the way, sent by God to be His presence in our lives, and to care for Mom as well as for me.

First, there were the people who saw Mom professionally: doctors, nurses, therapists, social workers. Many of them went beyond the call of duty—continuing to visit her, even after she had passed out of their area of specialization, checking on her progress and bringing smiles, hugs, little gifts, Scripture verses, and notes of encouragement.

There was Diane, the nurse case manager for the insurance company, who went the extra mile, making sure Mom got not just competent care, but the kind of care Diane would want for her own mother.

I saw Laura almost every day as she volunteered at the hospital information desk. She never failed to smile, wave, and call out, "I'm praying for your mom!" as I hurried past her station.

> I was hungry, and you fed me. I was thirsty, and you gave me a drink. I was a stranger, and you invited me into your home…I was sick, and you cared for me.
>
> —MATTHEW 25:35–36 (NLT)

I got to know Christine, who like me, was staying at the hospitality house to be near a loved one. She was there with her ten-year-old who had cancer, yet she still made time for the two of us to enjoy ice cream and late-night conversation together.

There were dozens of people online who left prayers, notes, and Scripture verses and who provided me with the comfort of knowing that whatever time of day or night, someone was remembering to pray for us.

I was "adopted" by congregation members from a couple of local churches, who provided meals, and rides to church, or any place else I needed to go, and who volunteered as visitors for Mom.

I got to know Tracey and Ryan, Pam and Tony's daughter and son-in-law. Tracey became my listening ear, and Ryan was my guardian angel—the one who introduced me to Miss Jean. Miss Jean was the lady who, for several months, provided me with not only a place to stay—but with a *home*, complete with hot meals, clean sheets, warm showers, and a stand-in mom.

GOD'S GIFT OF HEARING
— By Tez Brooks —

THERE ARE THREE tiny bones in the human ear that aid in sound transmittal—the smallest bones in the body. As delicate and important as they are, the human ears never get periods of rest. Even while sleeping, the ears can never turn off. Although hearing continues when people sleep, the brain does not process sounds the same as when awake. Whether conscious or not, softer noises still enter the ear but rarely wake a person unless it's loud enough to alert the brain and startle the individual in case of danger. The exquisite mechanisms of God's design are truly without number.

There were the people of Mom's home church. They were some of the most faithful to pray, write notes, and make phone calls. They traveled over an hour one way to visit Mom in the hospital and brought their kids' artwork—and their kids—because they knew how much Mom loved that kind of thing.

And finally, there were Pam and Tony—the ones who had started it all because they believed God had put them where they were for a reason, and because they listened to and obeyed the Holy Spirit, who sent them to be the presence of Jesus to my mom when she was all alone in the hospital.

A Hospice Blessing

By Teresa K. Lasher

The dad I knew was departing, and this aching, emaciated shell had taken his place. Only a week earlier, Dad sat in his favorite recliner playing UNO, winning more than once. He'd eagerly eaten turkey, after I'd cut it up for him, with gravy and mashed potatoes. I smiled thinking back to when he stuck out his tongue and said, "You can have my peas."

Now things were different. Around midnight, my sister Karen and I prayed that Dad would be relieved of pain. His labored, throaty breathing sounded as though he were drowning. Medication calmed his agitation temporarily. Why didn't the medications work as they were supposed to? *Lord, where are You?* We felt helpless. Every time he moved, he moaned and groaned. In the past, he rarely complained about pain.

Dad's mantra upon admission into assisted living almost three years ago was, "If I don't move it, I'll lose it." He consistently used his legs, arms, and walker to push himself all over the building and outside to the garden area in the sun. He'd travel to the dining room three times a day for meals, to the snack cart, and weekly bingo games. He loved car rides with us for family gatherings, ice cream, meals out, and doctor appointments until the pandemic hit and he was held captive inside four small walls. After fourteen miserable months in isolation, his mind, body, and soul gave up.

My sister and I sat near his bedside talking, playing songs such as "How Great Thou Art," "Amazing Grace," and "10,000 Reasons (Bless the Lord)." Reading Scripture out loud reminded us that He is our good Shepherd and all that we need.

I began praying, *If it be Your will, take him and let him join Mom so they can have that happy reunion. Let the confusion, pain, and suffering end. For his sake, please, God.*

I whispered in Dad's ear, "It's OK. You've fought the good fight. Mom's been waiting thirty years for you in heaven. You've done a good job." I kissed his bald head. "We'll miss you, but it's OK to go. Give her a big hug for us. We love you, Dad."

There was no response. He continued to breathe heavily and moan in pain whenever the nurses moved him.

Friday night Karen and I watched his blanket move up and down slowly at varying rhythms. At some point, we knew the blanket would stop moving. Saturday morning at 6:53 a.m., he passed from this life into the next.

Thank You, God, for healing Dad's wounds. His spirit is alive, well, and refreshed. He's so much better where he is.

In-the-moment decisions needed to be made. Since Dad had been in hospice, we'd already met with the funeral home, planned the type of burial, and gathered the death certificate data. I was thankful I'd handled that earlier—not in the midst of great emotional turmoil.

Due to COVID-19 limitations, the assisted living chapel was closed. Funerals were scarce. In the final stages of hospice care, we could make an appointment and remain in the room. We were thankful for small blessings.

The hospice team volunteered to come in and give a blessing of thanks service. After much deliberation, we agreed. I thought this event might be awkward and unpleasant. I was wrong. They asked my sister and me to choose a favorite shirt of Dad's and then leave the room for a while. We also picked a ball cap for him because he rarely was seen without one.

When they were ready for the service, they escorted us back into Dad's room. At first, I thought a miracle had taken place. The social worker and hospice sister had prepared his body, dressing him in his favorite, colorful, striped shirt and ball cap. They'd placed his hands around two red roses that my grand-daughter brought in the day before. From his earlier curled-up fetal position, he now looked as if he were merely resting peacefully. His face was calm and clean, with a bit of a smile curled about his lips.

The scent of lavender oil permeated the small, simple room. A stuffed Mickey Mouse from my daughter guarded Dad on his hospital bed. A nightstand/table held cards of cheer, a vase of fresh flowers, and a stuffed teddy bear from Karen. His mini-refrigerator sat between the bathroom and door leading to the outer hallway. This is where he stashed treasures to share with others to munch on later.

From Dad's open window, a gentle spring breeze drifted among us and throughout the room. This room would be the last place we'd see his earthly body and whisper, "I love you."

We cried tears of sorrow over losing him, and tears of joy realizing he was now with our mom. Dad was free from para-noia, pain, and years of confusion caused by dementia. Thoughts of heaven came to mind with the verse from Revelation 21:4 (NIV): "He will wipe every tear from their eyes. There will be no more death or mourning or crying or pain, for the old order of things has passed away."

The hospice women set up a video meeting allowing family members and friends to participate and watch the blessing service. My fifteen-year-old granddaughter sang "Amazing Grace," as we all chimed in together. We shared precious last words and notes of music. As we sang together, I felt God smiling on us, giving His approval and blessing.

The hospice sister gently placed small drops of lavender oil on various parts of Dad's body as she spoke. She pronounced a blessing of thanks over his eyes, mind, ears, mouth, hands, feet, and ended with his heart. Lastly, a prayer was offered: "May the angels of eternal life draw you into the embrace of God. May the angels of mercy comfort you and bring you peace as you depart from us. May the angels of hope take you by the hand and lead you home."

> **"For I know the plans I have for you," declares the LORD, "plans to prosper you and not to harm you, plans to give you hope and a future."**
>
> –JEREMIAH 29:11 (NIV)

Since both hospice women knew Dad from past visits, they spoke personally about Dad. The service didn't last long, but it was extensive in meaningfulness. Dad's blessing service surprised me by feeling natural, real, and right. After the service, we were invited to spend as much time as needed to say our goodbyes, or as I liked to think of this time as our "see you later" words.

"Do you have any questions?" asked the sister. "I speak at many services such as this. I can tell that you are a close family who really love your dad."

We nodded and she continued. "This doesn't happen all the time. What I see does my heart good."

Hugs and tears took the place of words.

Time to move on to the next steps. Our lingering longer would not change the facts. We selected a few memorable items and then took the next day off. Upon returning, we emptied his room, distributing a few items to family and donating the rest. Karen and I each chose one of his flannel shirts and a blanket. Dad's most prized article, his retirement badge encased in a protective cube, went to our brother.

> **Yes, we are of good courage, and we would rather be away from the body and at home with the Lord.**
>
> **—2 CORINTHIANS 5:8 (ESV)**

I found myself going through the motions as if in a trance. *Is this real or am I imagining it?* We relied on family members to navigate us through the next hours, days, and weeks. Gifts of food, words of encouragement, and prayer demonstrated that our family was loved.

Though much of the pandemic prevented visits, Dad received cards, notes, and gifts. We showered him with our prayers. I'm convinced he knew we cherished him during those long isolation periods.

Sometimes people blame God for a loved one's painful death. As I pondered the loss of Dad, his passing seemed too soon and unnecessary. If it weren't for the pandemic and forced isolation, would he still be here today? I don't know. I knew God meant no harm, but still my heart needed convincing. I needed to keep reading the promises written by the prophet Jeremiah.

What I learned about faith and family I learned from my mom. Not so much from what she said, but how she lived.

She prayed for us, wanting us to be kind to others and lean on God. God's spirit and truth lives on in their children and grandchildren.

Decades ago prior to the arrival of my first child, Mom pressed into my hand a 3-by-5 note card with these reassuring words: "Fear thou not; for I am with thee: be not dismayed; for I am thy God: I will strengthen thee; yea, I will help thee; yea, I will uphold thee with the right hand of my righteousness" (Isaiah 41:10, KJV).

The finality of not having an earthly father hit me hard. I was now an orphan, but I wasn't alone and had not been abandoned. I needed to trust my heavenly Father even in the darkest moments—*especially* in the dark moments. I also saw and felt His presence through my family and friends.

Dad passed from this life into a much better life. What more could we ask for? This is amazing grace. As long as I remember that God is with me wherever I go in the future months and years, life can be good. It's not goodbye but see you later.

Ordinary people accomplishing extraordinary things? Perhaps. But I'll go one better and suggest that we're all extraordinary in our own way, and that it's what we do with our extraordinariness that sets us apart and makes all the difference.

—Denzel Washington, actor

CHAPTER 7

Ordinary People Who Accomplished Great Things

Bad Day at Starved Rock

By Mary Kay Moody

The ringing phone jolted me awake. *Bad news comes with midnight calls.* Fear clawed at me as I lunged to answer. Our son, Karl, had gone on a day trip in the morning and hadn't been home at nine thirty when I went to bed.

I grabbed the receiver, hoping my husband wouldn't wake. "Hello?"

"Mrs. Moody?"

"Yes."

"County Sheriff's Depart—"

"What happened? Is my son hurt?"

"He's in jail."

I heard in slow motion. *Jail? He went hiking.*

"You need to come bail him out..."

His words coagulated into noise that didn't register.

"Well, can you?"

"Can I what?"

"Pick him up."

"Now?"

"Yes," he said slowly.

"But I...I don't know if I can drive that far." I was recuperating from a surgery that I'd hoped to postpone until I finished graduate school. The doctor's words, "The tumor's crushing your spinal cord," had changed everything. I only attended classes two days a week, and that alone necessitated bed rest to prevent overwhelming pain.

My brain shifted into gear. "He has a truck. Can't he drive himself?"

"He needs bail posted."

"Can I do that by credit card?"

"He still needs a ride." His words hit like hammers.

I trembled and dropped onto a chair. "Why? Is he hurt?"

"Not so's he couldn't drive. Look, we can't release him until you arrive."

My mental gears spun. "You're not making sense."

"Want me to tell him you're not coming?"

"No! Tell…Why isn't he calling? He's allowed a call."

"No, ma'am, can't use the phone."

More brain gears engaged. "What about Smokey? You have his dog?"

"What dog?"

"His Siberian Husky! What did you do with the dog when you picked up Karl?"

"Lady, we don't have any dog. No dog mentioned in the report. I have to go. So, you're coming?"

"Yes," I whispered, then cradled the phone, struggling to wrap my mind around his nonsensical words. Karl and Smokey were inseparable. He'd rescued the pup when it was barely larger than a box of tissues.

I woke Ed and we left. When we arrived at the brick jail surrounded by police cars, I shuddered.

The foyer was poorly lit. At the triple-thick window's mini-porthole, Ed paid the bail. And we waited. Finally, Karl emerged, pale and silent. We hugged him, then took papers from the policeman, who turned and walked away.

"Wait!" I scurried after him. "I need his keys."

He turned, shaking his head. "His truck was towed."

"Towed where?"

"The duty sergeant'll give you a number, but you'll have to call tomorrow, lady." The tyrant rolled his eyes. "The tow guy ain't there in the middle of the night."

I bit my lip to keep from screaming.

In the car Ed said, "You'll be glad to get home."

"Home?" Karl bellowed. "You're going home?"

"Uh, yeah. It's nearly two. I leave for work at six."

"Let me out," Karl said through gritted teeth. "Smokey fell over a cliff. Those guys arrested me while I was trying to rescue him." His voice cracked. "Alive or dead, I'm not leaving him to be attacked by coyotes. Just drop me off."

I groaned. So often these two engaged in a battle of wills. Ed needed sleep; Karl wouldn't leave Smokey. Yet how could we search forests, cliffs, and canyons in the pitch-black November night?

"I know exactly where we were. It's not far off the road. I'll tell you where to stop."

Thirty minutes and myriad curves later, we pulled onto the shoulder. Karl opened the door.

I squeaked, "Honey, you can't walk off into the woods. You'll lose sight of us within 10 yards."

"I know what direction to go and how to get back."

"You said Smokey fell over a cliff. Are we above or below it?"

"Above."

"Then one wrong step and—"

"Look, Mom," he growled. "It won't take long. Either he's alive and walks out with me, or he's dead and I carry him home to bury."

"Grab the flashlight," Ed said. "I'll go too."

They tied a rope to the car and uncoiled it as they walked. "Please, God, keep them safe." I don't think I even prayed about Smokey; Karl believed the fall had killed him.

I endured the twenty minutes they were gone replaying the scenes Karl described of his afternoon. He and Smokey had followed a creek meandering through the woods. The trail narrowed above a canyon. Smokey stepped close, looking down. A mass of wet leaves slid, carrying the dog over the cliff, yelping as he fell the 40 feet.

> The LORD is good, a strong refuge when trouble comes. He is close to those who trust in him.
>
> —NAHUM 1:7 (NLT)

Karl crept to the edge and peered over.

Smokey lay motionless.

As Karl raced to his truck, he lost his footing crossing the creek and fell in. He reached his truck soaked and shaking uncontrollably. Knowing about hypothermia, he pulled his sleeping bag around his shoulders, cranked up the heater, then raced down the road asking everyone he passed for a rope or to call park rangers for a rope. Evidently someone called—but not for assistance. Karl encountered a sheriff's roadblock before he ever found help or a rope. He stopped, tried explaining the situation, and asked for help. The rangers just wanted him out of the truck.

"I don't need to get out. Just get a rope. Please, my dog's hurt and needs help."

"Just get out."

He refused.

They reached to open his door.

Without thinking, Karl locked the door, backed up, bypassed them on the shoulder, and continued his search.

And I am certain that God, who began the good work within you, will continue his work until it is finally finished on the day when Christ Jesus returns.

—PHILIPPIANS 1:6 (NLT)

Eventually officers boxed in his truck, sliced his seat belt, yanked him out, pepper sprayed him in the face, and arrested him.

That was at two in the afternoon. Why it took them until near midnight to call us was unknown—and an outrage. *My men shouldn't have to make a hazardous trek in the middle of the night.* I wanted to make somebody pay.

One step at a time, God said to my spirit.

"Please, Lord. Guide them away from slippery spots. Keep them from following Smokey over the cliff." I chewed my lip to stem the tears.

I heard their voices before they emerged from the woods, coiling the rope. Without the dog.

In the car, Karl slanted his head away from me and said, his voice cracking, "We scanned the canyon floor. He wasn't there."

"Does that mean—"

"We don't know what it means!" Karl screamed.

Ed eased onto pavement. "Either he woke up and walked away, or someone found him."

"Or something," Karl whispered.

We were quiet as we rolled through the gloomy night. I feared the consequences of Karl's rash decision and distress over Smokey might overwhelm him and cause him to doubt God's love and presence. His relationship with God was so fragile at that time. I begged God to comfort my son, strengthen us, and guide us through the challenges ahead.

The next day when Karl got home from work, he and I drove back to Starved Rock State Park. He searched the canyon again. We spoke with lodge employees, contacted animal control. Park Service said they would alert rotating maintenance crews, but a team wasn't due in that area for weeks. Again we drove home silent. And without Smokey.

Wednesday morning I cried my way through classes wondering if we'd be able to keep Karl home on Thanksgiving Day, and how we'd fare with him facing charges while the police denied they knew anything about a dog.

Wednesday afternoon, Karl insisted on going back. I decided to go with him. We retraced our steps. Still no word. As dinnertime neared, I called Ed.

"Mary, park service phoned. Smokey's OK."

"Karl!" My scream brought him running. "Smokey's alive."

We scribbled the phone number of the hikers who'd spotted him and got directions to their motel. We picked up some turkey soup, the quickest nourishing thing we found at the burger joint that an injured dog could eat. When we knocked on the door, it sprang open.

Smokey's howl-yodel that always sounded like talking greeted us. He limped over. He seemed as if half his life had drained away. Smokey *never* moved slowly.

GOD'S GIFT OF TOUCH
— By Lawrence W. Wilson —

WALKING OUTDOORS IS a great way to appreciate the miracle of God's creation. Sight is the primary sense at work, but touch can reveal even more beauty. By laying a hand on a tree trunk, the bark brings a sense of connection to the earth. Dipping a finger into the icy stream brings appreciation for its gentle power, and for the hardiness of creatures living there. Feeling the sun's relentless heat brings a sense of human frailty and vulnerability.

The family recounted how they'd noticed him lying near their path and turned around, unsure if he was tame. Smokey slowly rose and followed them. When they reached their car, he stood at the father's knee as if expecting the man would know what to do. They checked with a park employee and learned about our notices, so they helped the dog into their vehicle and fed him milk while they waited for us.

We thanked them and strolled to our car. I grabbed the soup. "Smoke, you hungry?" He licked the outside, then slurped up every drop before I could pour it into his bowl.

As we drove home, Smokey slept, his head in Karl's lap. Karl and I talked about how events had to mesh in order for us to have been reunited with Smokey. Acknowledging how God engineered those circumstances reassured us that He'd walk us through the ordeals ahead. And on that Thanksgiving Day, we were especially thankful we were together and safe.

Comforting Hugs

By Sandra Johnson

"She's gone," my brother-in-law Simon cried out on the other end of the phone.

"What?" I walked outside to the breezeway to get out of range of the kids' clinic where I worked as a nurse.

"Cindy's gone! She had a blood clot. They found her in the SUV with her seat belt in place. A jogger noticed her and called the police." Simon cried. The love of his life, my twin sister, was dead.

She's gone? The words echoed in my brain, but my heart couldn't hear it, couldn't bear it! My whole life seemed to turn upside down. I lost my identity in that moment when I lost Cindy. I felt like a wrecking ball hit my body and my heart cracked into a million pieces. Something exploded in my head, and I couldn't hear the cars passing the church or the kids' voices from down the hall. Clutching my cell phone, I slumped to the cold concrete and moaned.

"You need to drive to Prescott and tell your mom and stepdad." Simon's voice cracked.

Darkness seemed to swallow me. My legs felt like lead; my energy drained out through my toes.

"Why, God. Why her? Why now?" I sobbed. *Four months ago, I surrendered my life to You, turned everything back over to You,*

repented, took a new direction, and this is what You let happen? Why?
I don't understand.

I turned to my Bible. Jeremiah 29:12–13 (NIV) brought an answer: "Then you will call on me and come and pray to me, and I will listen to you. You will seek me and find me when you seek me with all your heart."

> For he has
> rescued us from
> the dominion
> of darkness and
> brought us into the
> kingdom of the
> Son he loves.
>
> —COLOSSIANS 1:13 (NIV)

I called a friend to drive me to my mom's house. My body still felt numb. We arrived an hour later in Prescott. A wave of nausea passed through me Mom opened the door and said, "Hi. I wasn't expecting you. What's up?"

"Cindy's gone. They found her in her car." Mom began to wail and grabbed me and held me tight. We both cried on and off for hours until we were exhausted. Charlie, my stepdad, waited patiently, offering tissues and water. The next day we planned the funeral.

It was summer, so I was on break from teaching nursing school. In the following days and weeks, I felt utterly alone. Waves of despair overwhelmed me. I lay in my bed under my blankets, unwilling to move. I lived in my pajamas, and I didn't eat or shower. I didn't talk to anyone or go shopping. I wanted to die, and I cried constantly.

During this time, I came down with a severe case of bronchitis. I coughed so hard that the muscles in my abdomen and ribs ached. I only communicated with my doctor about my illness and medications. None of my friends or neighbors or colleagues knew about my sickness.

Until August. After not interacting with anyone for weeks, I decided to visit my friend Lou. However, once there in front of her house, I sat in my car for twenty minutes. I still didn't want to deal with Cindy's death, I but felt a compulsion to tell my friend.

I heard her dogs barking before I knocked. She opened the door and a scent of peanut butter cookies floated in the air. She grabbed two mugs when we went into her kitchen and sat down. Before she poured some coffee, she pulled her chair close to me and stared into my eyes. I sat in silence. I knew my eyes were swollen and my clothes crumpled. My hair hadn't been combed for days.

"You've been crying," she said.

"Yes. Something terrible happened."

"What's going on?" She placed her hand on mine, eyes focused on my red, puffy face.

"Remember I told you I had a twin sister when you told me about your twin brother?"

"Yes" she said. "What happened?"

"My twin sister passed away."

"Oh no! Sandy, I'm so sorry." She grabbed me, and I melted into her shoulder. Without saying a word, she just held me for a long time in an extended hug. Finally, I gave a few details. I shared about how I didn't get to say goodbye and how my heart was broken because she was alone when she died. A little later, Lou mentioned a church in town that had a support group, a place for people to talk about their losses. She thought I should consider going to it.

"Don't know if I'm ready, but if I have time, I will. Thanks," I said as I prepared to leave.

The first night I walked into the fellowship hall for the support group, Anita, a gray-haired lady with dark-rimmed glasses, greeted me warmly. She escorted me to a round table with chairs. I saw other folks there with red, swollen eyes. Tissue boxes sat in strategic spots and chocolates were scattered in the middle of the tables. *Add chocolate and they will come.*

We were asked to introduce ourselves. I wanted to run out because the lump in my throat grew bigger as it came closer to my turn.

"I'm Sandy and my twin sister died in May due to a blood clot."

I felt like yelling, *I'm only half here; when she died, I died!*

> **In the same way, there is more joy in heaven over one lost sinner who repents and returns to God than over the ninety-nine others who are righteous and haven't strayed away.**
>
> **—LUKE 15:7 (NLT)**

God, how can I be sitting here? How can I speak? Don't You see? Tears flowed down my cheeks.

The first thirteen weeks of the grief program, I cried. The second thirteen weeks, I actually filled out our workbook, which had daily activities and encouraged us to read the Bible. A variety of scriptures about sorrow and God's grace and presence jumped off the pages and reached into my fractured heart. Healing began. I actually started speaking to the others in the program. The Holy Spirit began to mend the pieces of my heart. It felt miraculous.

Two years have passed since Cindy's death, and while I have had many sorrowful moments, I still have seen evidence of God with me. I remember one Sunday in church when I was feeling really sorry for myself. During worship time, instead of praying, I silently screamed at God.

I felt terribly alone. Even in a room full of believers, my loneliness seemed deafening. I yelled at God about being lonely. Why did Cindy have to die?

Suddenly, on the right side of my body, I felt a warmth start from the top of my head and move down to my waist. It reminded me of syrup dripping over a stack of pancakes. Warm and soothing.

I had no idea where this warmth, this feeling of comfort, was coming from. I looked up but saw no one near me, so the sudden sensation wasn't from a supportive friend. I bowed my head and closed my eyes again. In my mind, I saw my Savior ease off His throne and slide into the seat beside me. He tapped me on the shoulder, and, as I turned, He enveloped me in a hug.

I dug into my purse for a tissue and left the sanctuary. It was time for me to go to the church nursery, where I was signed up to care for the toddlers.

As I entered the doorway, I felt two little arms wrap themselves around my leg. I looked down. A blond-haired three-year-old I didn't know laid his head against my leg. After thirty seconds he let go. More tears fell from my eyes, my shoulders slumped, and my knees felt weak. I grasped the nearby counter.

"Mrs. Johnson, I'm sorry. Are you OK? Do you want me to take over your shift?" asked Jessica, the mom of the boy who

GOD'S GIFT OF TOUCH
— By Eryn Lynum —

PLANTS ALWAYS REACH for sunlight. This "heliotropism" or "sun turn" is written into them. As morning's sun climbs above the horizon, there is a visible response from certain flowers. They eagerly unfurl tightly wrapped buds, stretching out their petals to receive the light. Some plants turn their stems to track the sun's journey across the sky. God tucked into His children a similar recognition of light. Jesus declared in John 8:12 (NKJV), "I am the light of the world. He who follows Me shall not walk in darkness, but have the light of life." Like the flowers, His followers turn toward the warmth of His light and follow in His path.

---

had given me the hug. "That's so strange," she said. "Colton never hugs anyone!"

My tears still streamed, yet my heart sang as I explained. "God used your son to give me a hug today," I added.

She nodded, her own eyes brimming with tears as she studied my face. She reached out and we hugged. I felt her tears on my cheeks. This gave me courage to dry my eyes and walk into the nursery and take care of those little ones.

That Sunday, I realized how precious I was to God. I felt so loved because my God came down to hug me. I know God is with us all the time, no matter how horrible we might feel. No matter how sad, He is there to listen and be our comforter.

Losing Cindy became a lesson with a blessing in disguise. God used her passing to draw me nearer to Him. As a way to share His comforting presence and healing hugs with others, I now facilitate my own grief group.

A Securely Tied God-Knot

By Donna Collins Tinsley

"Jonathan and Lyzz are having a wedding shower, and Patti wants us to bring a special Bible verse, something we have made, or something sentimental to us as a love gift for them. Do you have any ideas?" I asked my husband, Bill.

"I'll think about it," he said as he turned back to his computer.

Patti and Chuck were our longtime home-church family friends. Jonathan was their oldest son and we, as well as they, were so excited about the upcoming shower and wedding. Thinking of a love gift but also keeping in mind my lack of skills in the craft department, I hoped we would be able to give something special to them.

I started thinking about our own wedding as my mind wandered back over thirty years to when I first met Bill. It was stormy the day I met him, and there always seemed to be a storm of some kind in our lives.

First came the storm of infertility, when we prayed for seven years for me to become pregnant. Finally, eight years after we were married, we had a baby. We already had a three-year-old granddaughter born to my oldest daughter (from my first marriage), who was wrestling with a substance use disorder at that time. This painful dilemma resulted in our trying to care for not only our two children, but some of hers for a time.

We seemed to always put ourselves and our own relationship on the back burner, and our marriage went out the window. I remembered going to a women's retreat and the speaker, after hearing some of what we were going through, asked me, "Where is your relationship with your husband with all these grandchildren in and out of your lives? How are you finding time for him?"

> **I belong to my beloved, and his desire is for me.**
>
> —SONG OF SOLOMON 7:10 (NIV)

Her words stayed in my heart and mind all these years later. I realized Bill and I weren't being faithful to the word of the Lord, to truly *forsake all others* and deal with our own marriage relationship. Not that we didn't love each other or were not committed to an "until death do we part" sort of marriage. But the dailiness of life and family stresses had taken a lot of the sparkle out of our eyes. Our time for a happy marriage seemed long overdue.

Lord, please restore the love-light to our eyes and lives, I silently prayed. *Let us be like those sweet older couples I see, still loving each other and holding hands many years down the road. Please remind us of the happiness we had when we first met each other and the desires of our heart to have a happy, "normal" family and to raise our children in the ways of the Lord. These storms have come against us, but we know that Your Word is true and that You will work things together for our good in Your best timing. So, Lord, I leave our marriage with You to repair it as You see fit. Please renew us in Your love.*

Later I pondered the verse in Ecclesiastes about a three-strand cord: "Two people are better off than one, for they can help each other succeed. If one person falls, the other can reach out and help. But someone who falls alone is in real trouble. Likewise, two people lying close together can keep each other warm. But how can one be warm alone? A person standing alone can be attacked and defeated, but two can stand back-to-back and conquer. Three are even better, for a triple-braided cord is not easily broken" (Ecclesiastes 4:9–12, NLT).

> **And above all these put on love, which binds everything together in perfect harmony.**
>
> —COLOSSIANS 3:14 (ESV)

I researched the verse and found out about something called a God-Knot that is used in some wedding ceremonies. I wondered if we could incorporate it into our love gift for Jonathan and Lyzz for their upcoming wedding shower. I told Bill that we could probably get cords of the different colors used—purple, gold, and white—and braid a small God-Knot. The gold cords are to represent God being invited to the marriage, purple for the groom as he is subjected to the leadership of the Lord in the marriage, and white for the wife, who is a symbol of the purity of the Bride of Christ, the church that Jesus will someday return to claim.

"That's a great idea," he said. "I can sew the strands on a round gold ring and maybe we can frame it in a shadow box."

"I'll type out the scripture to put in with it." Suddenly just having a project to work on together seemed like fun. I checked out the fabric to use as a background and visited craft stores. Bill found a frame that was perfect.

We presented the God-Knot to Jonathan and Lyzz at the shower and they loved it. As I read them the scripture about the God-Knot, I looked over at Bill. In my heart I recommitted to finding things he and I could do together to restore the tie that binds.

Not long after that, I took Bill on a special night away from home and the children. As we walked from the hotel to the car to return home, he grabbed my hand. My vision of growing old together, still holding hands and being in love, returned to me. It's as if the intimate presence God blessed us with in the beginning of our marriage was renewed with a fresh glow.

Regardless of the storms and trials of our lives, the God-Knot has been securely tied around our marriage by the very presence of God himself.

A Prepared Place

By Alice Burnett

"There is no accommodation in Bratislava," Pastor Novak announced pessimistically. On this trip to Czechoslovakia, one of my goals had been to find a place to live in the vast city—not an easy task for a family with three active boys.

My heart sank. I gazed across at buildings gray with the grime of years. Uniformly built concrete high-rise apartments towered over ancient structures in an old-fashioned, cobble-stoned street. No color broke up the drabness, not even advertising. My gloomy mood matched my surroundings. Even the sky, in April, was somber. An air of dejection hung over everything.

God had prepared my heart to come here. Years previously, He had promised that I would go to other countries on behalf of the Christian school movement we were involved in. And here I was, actually standing in the land of my parents' birth! I had traveled alone, scouting out the territory before our whole family would go to help a pastor start a Christian school, a concept formerly unheard of in this land.

"Behold, I am going to send an Angel before you to keep and guard you on the way and to bring you to the place I have prepared" (Exodus 23:20, AMP). I hugged this promise to myself.

There was no way I would have dreamed of doing this trip by myself. I had been excited and a little nervous, but now my shoulders slumped in defeat.

The bleak prospect of no accommodation was in stark contrast to the upbeat meeting I had attended two days previously, when interested parents listened to the welcome news of a Christian school for their children. They had prayed for such an opportunity, which had so long been denied to them. Their dream was about to come true, but the reality hinged on our being able to live among them and demonstrate how to make this dream a reality.

> **Now faith is confidence in what we hope for and assurance about what we do not see.**
>
> —HEBREWS 11:1 (NIV)

"I can show you the YMCA," said a fellow Canadian. "Maybe accommodation there would do in a pinch."

The YMCA? I thought, *That doesn't seem very adequate for our needs.* I had to explore every lead, though.

"All right. Let's go and look at it."

We were shown a small room. It looked comfortable enough. A washing machine was available, and a green space across the street would be a perfect play area for the boys. I was doubtful about the size of the room but made a reservation anyway for the end of August, when we hoped to arrive. In my mind, though, I held out for a *real* apartment that would suit us better.

Back in my hotel room later, a tangle of thoughts and impressions crowded my brain. I paced the floor in despair, wondering if this trip was nothing more than a huge mistake. There didn't seem to be any realistic way our plans would work. I thought of sending my husband, Terry, a message:

"Accommodation unavailable." All of a sudden, I stamped my foot and shook my head.

"No! God, You told me You had a place for us." I remembered the scripture about the angel and the prepared place. "The place *You* have prepared, Lord."

Would I depend on my eyes and ears and feelings? Or would I trust in God's promise to me? I was ready to battle my negative thoughts.

"You sent me here, Lord, and I will trust You!" I announced.

Speaking these words out loud helped. Faith pierced the darkness of my unbelief. I experienced a glimmer of hope. "I don't know how You'll do this, Lord, but I'm waiting for Your plan."

As Pastor Novak took me to the bus depot, I clung to my hope. At the last minute, just before I boarded the bus, he was frank with me. "We're not sure yet if we will sign the contract." I didn't know what to think.

Seated on the bus, I had to pray to calm my racing thoughts. *Was this whole trip in vain? What about Your promise to me, Lord?* It was hard to figure out in my head, but slowly, as the bus rolled on toward Prague, I remembered: He had brought me to the place He had prepared. I had to hang on to that.

Back home in Canada, though, it was hard to hang on to my faith. "Did God really say He would prepare a place?" Satan mocked me. I had to continually remind myself of the truth.

I had a wild idea one morning. In faith, I boldly marched in the May Day parade, wearing the Slovak national costume my mother had when she was young. My pastor and I carried a big banner, which read: *Christian Schools for Czechoslovakia.* What a stirring moment! My dream was on again.

While I was encouraged that day, it was hard to be enthusiastic as the days and months went by. We finally got the green light to go—the pastor on the other side of the world had signed the contract. We were on!

I started to pack in earnest. A teacher would rent our house. Finally, eight bulging suitcases sat by the door, holding what we thought we would need for a year.

> **And my God will meet all your needs according to the riches of his glory in Christ Jesus.**
>
> **—PHILIPPIANS 4:19 (NIV)**

On the day we were leaving, I checked each room again. All that was left in the study was our telephone, sitting forlornly in the middle of the floor, to be disconnected at the end of the day. In one hour, we would leave the house for our big adventure. *Brring!* The ring of the telephone pierced the silence. I answered but couldn't make out who was calling. *Oh! Someone from Bratislava!*

"We have an apartment for you!" The voice triumphantly described the apartment they had found for us. A living room. A large bedroom and two smaller bedrooms. A kitchen. A bathroom with our own washing machine and an adjacent water closet. A balcony where we could hang clothes to dry. Not only that, but all the furniture, bedding, dishes, and kitchen utensils were included. Even the heat and electricity were part of the month's rent. It was less than the rent we were asking for our house in Canada!

God had answered my prayer with an apartment according to Ephesians 3:20 (AMP) "… superabundantly more than all that we dare ask or think." I burst into happy tears.

My Lord *had* prepared a place for us all along.

God Sees and Knows My Heart

By Debra Shelton

I felt scared, confused, and hopeless as I sat on a bench in the London twilight. For over an hour, I had wandered the side streets trying to find the converted brownstone where I had reservations for my overnight stay, but the fingers of gray fog wrapped around the rows of look-alike buildings.

I couldn't seem to make my mind work. The stabbing, searing pain on the right side of my head overwhelmed me. I wanted to scream. Instead, I blubbered into my coat sleeve and hoped no one would notice.

Finally, I sucked in a ragged breath. I was now officially home-less, jobless, and almost penniless, with only a suitcase of clothes to my name. *How could you let this happen to me?* I asked God.

I had been obedient when God had put the call in my heart to go to Zambia. He'd given me a special verse, Isaiah 58:10 (NIV): "And if you spend yourselves in behalf of the hungry and satisfy the needs of the oppressed, then your light will rise in the darkness, and your night will become like the noonday."

With confidence and excitement, I'd sold my business, my home, and all my belongings to travel alone to a strange and challenging place. Even the fact that I was forty-nine years old didn't deter me. I put everything I had into caring for the children who came to the orphanage and school. Every day presented new challenges and adventures that made me feel vibrantly alive and more committed to sharing God's love. The wild beauty of the African bush, the smiles and laughter of "my" kids, and the generosity of the native people soon filled me with joy, love, and a sense of fulfillment.

> **Keep your heart with all vigilance, for from it flow the springs of life.**
>
> —PROVERBS 4:23 (ESV)

Then the headaches started. They swooped in, leaving me writhing in indescribable pain. On days when I couldn't function, I curled up on my bed in misery and tried not to think about everything that wasn't getting done.

I went into the city seeking help from local doctors, but lacking equipment, their diagnoses were mere guesses, including the one from Dr. Morgan, a young South African woman who cared for the children's health needs.

"I want you to fly down to Johannesburg and see a neurologist. You can stay with my family." She took my hand in both of hers. "I don't want to scare you, but this could be a tumor or an aneurysm. You need to get a proper diagnosis and care."

Instead of accepting her generous offer, I opted to return to the familiar surroundings of home. Now her words came back to me as I huddled on the cold London bench. Anger bubbled up. As concerned as I was about my health, I was more upset about having to leave Zambia and the children I loved. Who would care for them?

How could you let this happen, God? I opened my heart and now it's breaking into a million pieces.

My anger propelled me off the bench and down the sidewalk. Within minutes, I stumbled onto my accommodations. Disheartened, I checked in and staggered up the steep steps to my second-floor room, where I fell into bed for a few hours of sleep before continuing my journey back to the United States.

The morning dawned gloomy and damp. Mercifully, my head didn't hurt and my vision was clear. I dragged my suitcase and backpack to the closest Tube station and headed to Heathrow. Ten and a half hours later, I landed in Denver with mixed emotions.

I was home. Well, almost—I still had to get to the other side of the Rockies. I exited customs to find my mom and dad excitedly waving to me.

"Honey, we're so glad you're home!" My mom hugged me while Dad grabbed my bags. I read the relief on their faces. How could I tell them I might be dying of brain cancer? I couldn't and I wouldn't.

During the five-hour drive over the mountains, I sat in the back seat, exhausted, pretending to sleep to avoid their questions. Anxiety ramped up as I thought about the challenges I faced. My snowbird parents offered me their house as they were headed off to the warmer climes of Arizona, so at least I had shelter.

Still, I would need to pay for food and utilities, but how could I do that when I could barely function? How would I manage a job when pain blinded me and left me limp? Then there were the medical costs of figuring out if I had a brain tumor. Coming home seemed more terrifying than moving to the other side of the world had been!

During the following weeks, I visited a variety of doctors, including a neurologist who bluntly said nothing was wrong with me that a visit to a psychiatrist wouldn't cure. I was devastated and apparently crazy, but I didn't give up. Someone had to have the answers.

Meanwhile, my headaches worsened, and my weakness increased.

When my vision seemed to plunge, I went to see my eye doctor. He noticed my right eye was bulging from its socket. "Something is going on behind your eye. I can't tell precisely what, but it could account for your headaches. I think your primary doctor needs to order some specific tests."

"But I've already had an MRI and CAT scan. They said there are lesions in several places but nothing to account for the headaches and pain."

Dr. Ford removed his glasses. "I think you might have unwanted guests."

"What do you mean?"

Using a piece of silk, he cleaned each lens of his glasses and positioned them back on his nose. "From everything you've told me and from what I can observe, I think you may have picked up parasites. I'm surprised no one has ordered tests to rule them out."

I cringed at the thought of some kind of creepy-crawlies living inside me.

Parasites? It made sense. After all, I'd lived in the jungle where I had to boil my water before I drank it, and I'd seen what putzi and tsetse flies could do to humans and animals. Why hadn't any of the eight doctors I'd seen thought of that?

> **Know therefore that the LORD your God is God; he is the faithful God, keeping his covenant of love to a thousand generations of those who love him and keep his commandments.**
>
> **—DEUTERONOMY 7:9 (NIV)**

I went to Dr. Cramer, my primary care physician. "I'll run the tests, but they're very expensive," she said. "Knowing your circumstances, that's probably why none of the other doctors ordered them."

I tried not to focus on the fact that my being jobless was why no previous doctors even suggested the tests. If I did, I'd boil with anger. "How many tests?"

"Three. If the tests prove positive for parasites, we'll give you a series of drugs that should kill them, but the medicine is not cheap."

I took a deep breath and stood. "Let's do it. I want these things out of me. Even if it takes every dime I have."

The tests confirmed I had three different kinds of parasites. They caused the lesions in my brain and my eye problem. They had also invaded my stomach and intestines, wreaking havoc that would follow me for years.

Although I felt vindicated that I wasn't crazy, Dr. Cramer warned me that my compromised system meant I'd never be able to live in that kind of tropical environment again. So I couldn't go back to the children and the place I'd grown to love, where I felt useful and alive. I'd never get to see the end results of my work.

I shared my disappointment with a friend who later sent me a card. Inside, she wrote, "God is not unjust; he will not forget your work and the love you have shown him as you have helped his people and continue to help them" (Hebrews 6:10, NIV). She added, "He sees you and knows your heart."

That sentiment caused me to remember little Miss Mary, one of my orphans, who would say, "I see you, Mama" before climbing into my arms. I've come to know that God sees me. And more than anyone, He understands, comforting me with His sweet presence.

We all have angels
whispering in our ears
to reach up, to reach out,
to reach our greatest
potential. All we have
to do is listen.

—Jane Seymour, actor

CHAPTER 8
Angel Interventions

Invisible and Invincible!

By Heather Rodin

The deafening whir of the evacuation helicopter announced its arrival. With heavy hearts we hugged our twenty-five Haitian staff members and the many friends who had come to say goodbye.

Across the top of the compound wall and iron gates, village kids crowded together to wave and shout their goodbyes. It was time. We quickly grabbed our hastily packed bags and ran to climb aboard the chopper.

It was February 19, 2019, and Haiti was imploding. The stench of fear and evil paralyzed the country as violent uprisings drew world attention. Our presence at "Hope Grows Haiti" mission put our Haitian team in danger, and we knew we had to leave. But roads were blocked, and this helicopter was our only chance to get to the airport for the last flight out.

Havoc continued to reign in Haiti over the next two years with the arrival of COVID-19, political uprisings, an earthquake, a hurricane, the president's assassination, and over 1,000 kidnappings and murders. This beautiful country was in turmoil like never before.

Our staff was physically and emotionally exhausted. The spirit of fear had incapacitated all but a few in mission leadership, and our field director, Willy, sounded desperate in his message to us.

"It is so difficult with such days in Haiti now. We rely on your spiritual support more than ever. Please pray for us so we keep our focus on Jesus. Pray for our Lord to banish our fear!"

So my husband and I prayed those exact words. We also made a call to a few faithful prayer warriors to bring our mission and staff before almighty God and intercede on their behalf, claiming 2 Timothy 1:7 (NASB): "For God has not given us a spirit of timidity, but of power and love and of discipline."

We know God hears the prayers of His children. We know He's a God of love, compassion, and mercy. But what a thrill the day we saw Him move in a miraculous way, showing His presence, power and majesty!

We had been asking Jesus to make our team invisible to the enemy, especially when they needed to go to the bank to draw out each month's funds for payroll, medical supplies, and food for the feeding program that fed around 300 kids each day. With the growing number of armed and dangerous gangs on the prowl, this had become a real concern. Many people were being robbed and killed outside of banks. The danger for our staff was immense.

So, we prayed similarly to what Elisha prayed when he asked God to open the eyes of his scribe to see the forces of heaven ready to fight for them: "Then Elisha prayed, and said, 'LORD, please, open his eyes so that he may see.' And the LORD opened the servant's eyes, and he saw; and behold, the mountain was

> For it is written, "He will command his angels concerning you, to guard you."
>
> —LUKE 4:10 (ESV)

full of horses and chariots of fire all around Elisha" (2 Kings 6:17, NASB).

> **So you will walk in the way of the good and keep to the paths of the righteous. For the upright will inhabit the land, and those with integrity will remain in it.**
>
> —PROVERBS 2:20–21 (ESV)

So, although we asked for invisibility, we also petitioned God to make His warrior angels visible to the enemy.

One day we saw how powerfully God answers our prayers.

Willy and his assistant, Moses, had just gone to the bank to withdraw a large sum of money. It was enough to see them through an extended period of time. As Willy left to make the arrangements to pick up food, Moses pocketed the money and went to get the car. Suddenly two gang members appeared in front of him with guns pointed at his head.

"Give us the money!" they shouted.

Moses froze, knowing this would probably end in death, even if he willingly handed over the money. The heat of the day now felt like fire, and his body broke into a tremendous sweat. He was shaking and couldn't speak, but silently called on God.

Before the men with guns could shoot, a voice was heard—clear and firm.

"Hey, guys! You cannot do that here!"

The two would-be robbers stared at something just behind Moses's right shoulder. With stricken expressions, they turned and fled.

Moses was left standing there, money still in his pocket and no bullet wound in his body. Still shaking, he turned to thank the Good Samaritan for coming to his rescue, but no one was there. He searched the buildings in case someone had shouted out a window, but they were too far away and would not have been heard. It appeared he stood alone.

How was this possible? So many times people robbed outside a bank were shot and killed. What had made the robbers turn and run like that? Normally they would just shoot anyone who challenged them. But no shot had been fired—and Moses was walking away, safe and free. Where had that voice come from?

As he slowly continued down the street, truth dawned like a morning sunrise. God had placed an angel by his side—perhaps a warrior angel with a flaming sword. He had not seen the heavenly being, but obviously, the enemies had.

Moses's steps became light, and his heart almost burst. He had just experienced a miracle! An answer to prayer! God had walked with him, watching over him even when he was not aware. The presence of God was real, tangible, and trustworthy.

As Moses spotted Willy approaching, he felt joy bubble up and hurried to share his incredible experience.

The two men returned to the mission compound, praising God for His matchless grace and mercy and telling everyone they could. We were immediately contacted and listened with hearts overflowing to a recounting of what we unquestionably knew to be answered prayers. The enemies' eyes had been opened to see a member of God's great angel army protecting His children.

Haiti continues to roil in struggles, but I know that God is present amid the danger and distress. And He sends angels to prove It.

My Angel on the Psych Ward

By Katie R. Dale

I was only sixteen when my parents had me hospitalized in a juvenile psych ward. I was diagnosed with bipolar disorder type one with psychotic features. Medications and therapy kept me stable for eight years. Then at twenty-four, I errantly believed I was healed. I went off my medications and ditched the therapy.

Pleading to leave the psych ward after I had admitted myself voluntarily was part of the effects of the illness. That and the fact that when you're crammed into a hospital unit with forty other patients with mental illness, you're bound to lose it a bit. I lost it a lot. I acted out, primarily out of uninhibited instincts due to the imbalance of my brain chemistry.

The brain, will, emotions, and spirit are all interconnected. Because my brain wasn't functioning normally, everything else in my life followed suit. My emotions were ravaged, and any level of comfort seemed foreign. My eating habits deteriorated. I felt abandoned. Between the ambiguous communication from the hospital and my frame of mind, the projected eleven-day stay felt like an indefinite sentence.

No visitors came to see me except my husband. Having moved to another state shortly after I married my husband three years prior, I received no phone calls except from my family, who were now a thousand miles away. No flowers were sent and no friends or family made meals for my husband. I felt deserted, disrespected, and most of all, disbelieved. I wanted desperately for someone to believe me.

The light at the end of the tunnel dimmed. The ambush on the mind was too great for me to bear—I lost control of all threads of sanity. I figured this was the price I had to pay for going off my medications.

Enter a mysterious stranger. As I endured another trial medicine and treaded water in the waves of manic psychosis, she appeared. Portraying another patient, she came to me in the personal appearance of an angel: curly golden hair, emerald eyes, a heart-shaped face, cream-colored turtleneck, and white-and-gold-flecked cotton skirt. While I can't guarantee she was an actual messenger from God, she sure acted like one. In my desperation and with my secure faith, I couldn't deny the potential for a miracle in the midst of my mess.

> ## Deliver me from my enemies, O God; be my fortress against those who are attacking me.
>
> —PSALM 59:1 (NIV)

While I was flailing my arms about and having a fit of explosive behaviors, fellow "patient" Carrie Nagle approached me. I had never noticed her before. She escorted me to my bedroom off the hallway and closed the door behind us.

"You need a break. I get it," she whispered.

As we walked to the center of the room, I dropped to my knees, and she followed. I buried my head in my hands and released the sobs I couldn't hold in. As she wrapped her arms around me, I sensed that she might well be my guardian angel. Just rearranging the letters of her last name spelled out *angel*.

She must have picked up on that unspoken notion, gently affirming my thoughts, because she said, "Have you heard of the guardian angel prayer?"

> **Are they not all ministering spirits sent out to serve for the sake of those who are to inherit salvation?**
>
> —HEBREWS 1:14 (ESV)

I had been taught in church and at home not to pray to angels or revere them at the level of God. But I listened as she recited the prayer in earnestness, putting my cares above her own concerns.

I marveled at how she picked up on the guardian angel concept and seemed to play the role when I asked her personal questions about whether she'd been at my birth and by my side ever since. She acknowledged she had, and, as I gazed into her deep, gemstone eyes, I envisioned her sitting in front of the throne of God, gold-flecked skirt spread around her, hands in pleading form, communing with God.

Granted, she was possibly another patient, not my actual guardian angel. But the fact that she came to me and comforted me at my worst was the best thing that could have happened. She was like an ambassador from God who reminded me that even in this place where I was forsaken by medical professionals, I wasn't forsaken by Him.

After Carrie came alongside me during my breakdown, my time inside the ward was more bearable. The days were more tolerable, and the nights were not so scary and threatening because Carrie was there. Her sheer presence made me more prone to laugh and experience this proverbial medicine for the

GOD'S GIFT OF TOUCH
— By Lawrence W. Wilson —

IN THE BIBLE, the laying on of hands is associated with receiving the Holy Spirit (Acts 8:14–19), conferring authority (1 Timothy 4:14), and healing (Luke 4:40). Now research has shown the benefits of touch in the treatment of anxiety and depression, trauma recovery, and headaches. Touch facilitates consciousness states associated with alpha, beta, theta, and delta brain waves. It also stimulates circulatory, lymphatic, and immune responses, and regulates the respiratory rhythm. It can activate the release of endorphins, oxytocin, and serotonin, and reduces cortisol levels. Science now confirms what the apostles always knew. There is power in human touch.

---

soul. She taught me funny sayings to help lighten the atmosphere. With her by my side, I could inhale deeper. I could rest lighter. I slept soundly.

As hard as it was to be living in the psych ward in what seemed like a rational state of mind, I realized I needed to be there to get better. Perhaps I could have endured the hospitalization without Carrie, but I'm glad our paths crossed. She was a light in a dark place, ministering to my fractured mind amid so much confusion and chaos.

The best part was that she believed me. My troubled heart, my frightened mind, and my realities that may or may not have been real—she believed them too.

After returning to my medications and therapy, I began my journey back home and back to a sound mind, closer to God thanks to His angel named Carrie.

Art Angel

By Deryn van der Tang

I had come to Australia to visit my daughter, who had moved there a few years ago. I had investigated the process of applying for a permanent resident visa. However, I had just discovered that this was not going to be possible. No immigration law fitted my circumstances due to my age, finances, and recent work experience. I had been a widow for almost a year and had decided to move closer to my daughter as I did not want to be left in Cape Town in South Africa to grow old alone.

The wet and miserable day reflected my own sadness.

"I think I will just go into town and visit the art gallery," I said to my daughter as I picked up my purse and headed out the door. Art was always my solace, and the quietness of the gallery would suit my mood. I could be alone with my grief and thoughts. I climbed on the bus that took me to the Queensland Gallery of Art near the Brisbane River and headed for the entrance on arrival. After wandering around, I came to the level displaying old Renaissance-style paintings.

"Hello, do you know the story of that painting?" I looked up to see who was speaking to me. A slightly built, sandy-haired, middle-aged man looked at me through his round-framed spectacles.

"No," I said as I looked more intently at the painting in front of me. It was one of those medieval religious paintings depicting a saint or scene from the Bible.

"I am Barry," he said, and then he explained a few details about the painting. He then moved the conversation onto a much deeper spiritual level by talking about miracles. I was a little disconcerted and looked at him to see if he was perhaps mentally disturbed, but his pale-blue eyes seemed lucid and intelligent, so I listened.

> **For we are God's handiwork, created in Christ Jesus to do good works, which God prepared in advance for us to do.**
>
> —EPHESIANS 2:10 (NIV)

"Do you know the story of Moses crossing the Red Sea?" he asked.

"Yes," I replied. He talked in some detail about the flight of the Israelites from Egypt.

"The miracle was not necessarily the circumstances or the event," he explained, "but the timing of the circumstances and the event."

As soon as he said that, I knew he was speaking words of truth, a message. Tears started to flow down my cheeks as I understood that God had given him a message for me specifically. As he left, he turned and, pointing his finger at me, said, "God has said, I will never leave you or abandon you" (Hebrews 13:5, ISV). And then he was gone. I realized immediately that I'd just had an encounter with an angel.

At my daughter's home, I discussed the incident with her.

"Mom," she said, "I don't think you are meant to come to Australia, as much as we both would like it."

"I believe it was a message from God," I said. "There may be a right time, but it is not now. Let us wait on God and see what happens." My daughter agreed with me, and I returned to Cape Town.

Six months later, some old friends, Roger and Ann, whom I had known many years, from the church I grew up in, came to visit me. They were on vacation from England, and I told them of my dilemma with children living on three different continents. I explained that I decided to live in Australia, near my daughter, but could not get an Australian visa, and I did not want to stay alone in Cape Town.

"Why don't you apply for a job at Silver Leaf Homes?" Roger said. "I am a trustee there, and we are looking at taking on a new home to manage in Fordend, north of London. You would make an ideal candidate for a manager."

I thanked him and later wrote a letter to the CEO of Silver Leaf Homes, an organization that provides care and housing for the aged, headquartered in London. I asked for further information and wrote that I would be interested in a position. I received a standard acknowledgment of my letter, but nothing more. Months passed, and I gave up on waiting for a reply.

Then I planned a visit to my son who lived in London. I decided to write one more time to Silver Leaf Homes. I wrote that I would be visiting London at the end of May, and I would be available for an interview. They responded by saying they would like the opportunity to meet with me.

I set up a meeting at their London office and was interviewed by the human resources and care and housing directors.

"We are thinking about taking on a property in Fordend, about an hour north of London, that will require a manager, but it is still under negotiation, so we cannot offer you anything right now. But if you are interested, we will set up a meeting with the current manager so you can look around and see if it is something you would be able to do," they said. Although I had not managed a facility for the elderly before, I had managed a condominium block for fourteen years in Cape Town. I had adequate experience dealing with all the problems associated with buildings and the people living in them.

"I would love to visit Fordend," I replied.

The local housing manager for Fordend, a lovely, slightly younger lady, showed me around the buildings and introduced me to the staff and current trustee. The old Victorian houses were set in beautiful gardens, and there was a park with a pond across the road. As we enjoyed a cup of tea in the cozy wood-paneled dining room, discussing the duties and roles of the

> **And do not forget to do good and to share with others, for with such sacrifices God is pleased.**
>
> **—HEBREWS 13:16 (NIV)**

manager, I noticed paintings of African scenes on the walls, and they reminded me of home.

"A missionary from the Congo who stayed with us painted them," the trustee explained. I was starting to feel at home already. After I looked around the home, the housing manager sat down with me to explain that the current setup was not viable, and I would need to put in place management systems that would address the shortcomings of the present system. This would not be easy, as people are resistant to change.

"Well," she said, "can you do it?"

I drew my breath in sharply; here was where the rubber hit the road! If I said yes, my life would change forever. I would have to give up my lovely home in Cape Town. If I said no,

GOD'S GIFT OF SIGHT
— By Tez Brooks —

THE AMERICAN ANTELOPE is the second fastest land mammal after the cheetah. Their eyesight is keen because their peripheral vision reaches an impressive 320 degrees, making it almost impossible for predators to sneak up on them. When danger approaches, they are not built for fight, but for flight. This animal models something important to Christians. Mark 13:33 (NIV) reminds readers to "Be on guard! Be alert!" Believers aren't always meant to stand and fight the enemy. Often, their best chance of survival is to run—right into the arms of Jesus.

---

would I give up my only opportunity to be near one of my children and regret it for the rest of my life?

"Yes," I breathed—for better or for worse.

I returned home after my visit but was asked by Silver Leaf to come back to London for a second interview.

"The house is still under negotiation, so we cannot guarantee you the position until details are finalized. But, if we were to take it on, when would be the earliest that you could start working here?" the director asked.

"The earliest I could start would be October 1," I replied. "I need to see my current job through to the year-end audit."

"That is the date we had anticipated taking over the Fordend Home," the director responded.

The words of the "angel" Barry floated back to me: "It is not the event or the circumstance, but the timing of the event or circumstance."

This was, indeed, God going before me and making way for me to be near one of my children.

I went back to Cape Town to prepare for the move when the call came that I had the job. This was a miracle for someone who was already in her sixties. This was a time to rebuild a new life in a new country near my son. Whatever the challenges, I knew God would never leave me nor forsake me. The job was custom-made for me, and I knew that all would be well. Whenever I faced a difficult moment, I just thought of Barry's words and the years of preparation that had brought me to this place right on time.

Angel in the Hallway

By Marcia Lee Laycock

The phone call was not unexpected. After a long battle with dementia, my mom, who was in a hospital on the other side of the country, had quietly slipped into eternity.

Though I had known the day would come, it arrived when my life was already overflowing with stress and apprehension. I had just undergone chemotherapy and surgery for breast cancer and now was having weeks of radiation treatments. I had often felt God's presence as I went through the treatments, but this news was a heavy burden

The hospital near my home was not equipped for radiation, so I had to drive more than two hours to a cancer clinic in Calgary, Alberta, every Monday. I stayed with my daughter and son-in-law in the city as I went through the treatments during the week, then drove home on Friday afternoon.

I often used that driving time to pray for strength to get through the treatments, as well as for the many others going through the same thing in the huge treatment center.

The news about my mom left me numb and sad that I had not been able to be with her in her last days on this earth. But my spirit was lifted as I spent time with God, weeping as I sensed His presence.

My spirit was also lifted somewhat by another phone call that evening. A friend let me know that a mutual friend of ours was in town. She wondered if I could join them for dinner on Monday night after my radiation treatment. Though my weariness was almost overwhelming, I said yes.

The drive to the city the next day was even more stressful than usual as high winds blew falling snow across the highway. As my tires slid on icy patches, I slowed down and gripped the steering wheel.

"Please, God, keep me safe. Help me get to the clinic on time," I prayed. I was always conscious of getting to the clinic on schedule; they stressed punctuality because of the number of patients being treated every fifteen minutes in the radiation units. To my distress, I was a bit late when I pulled into the huge parking lot and had to circle several times to find a spot.

> This I declare about the LORD: He alone is my refuge, my place of safety; he is my God, and I trust him.
>
> —PSALM 91:2 (NLT)

I rushed into the clinic to discover that two units had broken down, throwing all the schedules off, so my appointment had been pushed back a few hours.

More time to spend in prayer, I decided.

When I was finally called for treatment, I discovered I would not be taken to the usual unit, where the nurses and technicians knew me. I groaned inwardly and whispered another prayer. I was learning what 1 Thessalonians 5:17 (ESV) means when it says, "Pray without ceasing."

Mondays were always difficult because that was the day new pictures had to be taken so the radiation could be targeted for the best effect. The nurse who normally positioned me was quick, a blessing since I had to remain still with my arms above my head—a terribly painful position.

The young assistant who tried to position me this time was obviously new at the job. Tortuous minutes ticked by as he tried to get my body and the equipment lined up correctly, shifting me around while I still held my arms painfully above my head. Finally, the radiation was applied, a process that only took a few minutes. But by the time it was over I was near tears from the pain.

The assistant gave me an apologetic look when he told me that all the nurses had gone home; no one else was around to do the usual post-radiation treatment. I groaned for real this time. It always felt so good to have the salve and bandages applied to the burns by skilled hands. The young man patted my shoulder. "I'll give you the cream and gauze to take home," he said.

I nodded but knew I could not do nearly as well as the nurses did. I sat to wait, sighing as the empty hallway echoed with his footsteps.

Lord, please. I can't take much more.

Was it a prayer or a complaint? I wasn't sure but I remembered a Scripture verse that said something about the Holy Spirit praying for us with "groanings that cannot be expressed in words" (Romans 8:26, NLT). I knew He was doing that for me in that moment, and my heart was comforted.

I glanced at my cell phone. I was already forty minutes late for the dinner appointment. I called to cancel, but my friends insisted I come anyway. The assistant returned with the gauze and cream, and I scurried toward the exit, still fighting tears.

I was about halfway to the doors when a nurse suddenly stepped out of a side room. She smiled as I approached, but I could not bring myself to return her smile. She stopped, cocked her head, and asked, "Are you OK?"

I burst into tears. The woman gently grasped my arm and led me to a bench. She put her arm across my shoulders as I sobbed. I regained control and told her I would just leave, since there was no one to apply the salve and bandages. She squeezed my shoulder and said, "Come with me."

She led me to a side room, and with gentle, skilled hands applied the cream and bound my wounds as she asked questions that coaxed out the rest of my story. By the time she was done, I felt so blessedly cared for and knew I had the energy now to keep going.

> **I know the LORD is always with me. I will not be shaken, for he is right beside me.**
>
> —PSALM 16:8 (NLT)

I blinked back tears as I headed for the exit again, wondering if an angel had just ministered to me. In the parking lot, the air was still, the sounds of the city muffled by the newly fallen snow. The sparkling cover of white glistened under the streetlights. I wept again, but this time with a newfound joy and peace that welled up inside me and gave me strength. I remembered a verse I had memorized years before: "I am leaving you with a gift—peace of mind and heart. And the peace I give is a gift the world cannot give. So don't be troubled or afraid" (John 14:27, NLT).

When I got to my friends' home they welcomed me with open arms and warm hugs. We enjoyed a lovely dinner, and, as I looked at their caring faces, I thanked God for them and for that stranger—or was it an angel?—who cared enough to take the time to help when things had seemed so grim.

A Battle for Souls

By Cindi Myers

I was battle-weary and prayer-weary the day I saw the giant
angel.

Prayer has always been easy for me. I always took to heart
the verse from 1 Thessalonians 5 to pray without ceasing. That
is until I was teaching Bible class to eighty-six middle school
students at a local Christian school.

I soon found out that teaching Bible class was not for the
faint of heart. Each time I held class, I was stirring the spiritual
pot. Each time a student responded to the gospel the spiritual
warfare amped up. I often felt like I had a bull's-eye on my back.

Just when I thought things could not get any harder, I
started my ninth year in the school. It quickly became brutal.
Many of the students struggled with their faith. Some wanted
to believe but could not find the courage to take the step of
faith in God, while others lashed out, saying God was just a
myth. Arguments broke out in the middle of class, pitting new
believers against those who didn't trust God.

I spent hours praying with those who shared their struggles
with me. I passionately interceded for those who didn't want
to talk, begging God to break down their walls and open their
eyes to see Him. The burden was oh so heavy.

As the year picked up speed, I wondered if my prayers were
doing any good. I saw anger and distrust in my students' faces.

I often told God that I just could not do it anymore. But then the Holy Spirit would whisper that He placed me there at that time, for those students, and that He was with me. So, I continued to pray.

My apprehension grew, and I feared the students would turn their backs on God permanently. About three months before the end of the year, several students were on the verge of accepting Jesus, but Satan and his followers were working just as hard to discourage them.

> **Be on guard. Stand firm in the faith. Be courageous. Be strong.**
>
> —1 CORINTHIANS 16:13 (NLT)

By this time in the year, the students should have solidified their relationships with one another and their teachers, leading to a certain amount of goodwill among the students. But for months, instead of being a place of welcome and peace, strife filled the halls of the school.

One Friday morning, as I pulled into the school parking lot, I asked God to give me insight, wisdom, and peace. I needed Him to lift my burden. I was not sure how much fight I had left in me.

As I gathered my supplies and left my car, I noticed almost all the other teachers had arrived. I hurried to the stairs at the middle school hall door, and I stopped in my tracks. There, in front of the door, was a man dressed in a white robe, standing about 9 feet tall. He held a golden sword that was at least 4 feet long. The light surrounding him shimmered.

I stared in awe.

"Only those I allow will enter this hallway—whether physically or spiritually," he said. I looked down at the stairs to make sure I wouldn't miss the next step as I moved forward, but when I looked back up at the door, the man had disappeared. As I gazed at the empty space, I was filled with peace.

> **For you know that when your faith is tested, your endurance has a chance to grow.**
>
> —JAMES 1:3 (NLT)

I walked to my classroom asking the Holy Spirit about what I had just seen. He told me I had just seen an actual angel. The angel was guarding the entire school but was remaining in the middle school area since that was where most of the spiritual battle was taking place. My thoughts went to Ephesians 6:12 and I reminded myself that the fight is not against flesh and blood, but against the rulers, against the authorities, against the world powers of this darkness, against the spiritual forces of evil in the heavens.

Later that day, one of my students came to speak with me. She explained that she had come to my room before school to talk with me, but I wasn't there. However, she saw an extremely tall man in a white robe with an enormous sword standing next to the board. The man did not speak to her.

I laughed with amazement when she told me. I then explained what had happened when I had arrived that morning. She was so excited that she had also seen the angel. For me, this was a confirmation of what I'd seen. It spurred me on to continue fighting for the students.

The spiritual warfare continued for about two more months, but I didn't give up. I reached out to other teachers, and we prayed, lifting each student to God's throne. Eventually, after much intercession, peace flooded the middle school hallways. God showed His power and faithfulness as He worked in the students' lives. By the end of the year, five students had committed their lives to Christ.

As the year closed, I felt as if I had been through a war. I smiled as I cleaned out my room for the summer, knowing that I was blessed beyond measure to have the privilege to wage war on behalf of the students who walked the middle school corridors. And thanks to the white-robed, sword-toting angel, I had proof that I would never fight in those halls alone.

A Note from the Editors

We hope you enjoyed *Strengthened by His Touch,* published by Guideposts. For over 75 years, Guideposts, a nonprofit organization, has been driven by a vision of a world filled with hope. We aspire to be the voice of a trusted friend, a friend who makes you feel more hopeful and connected.

By making a purchase from Guideposts, you join our community in touching millions of lives, inspiring them to believe that all things are possible through faith, hope, and prayer. Your continued support allows us to provide uplifting resources to those in need. Whether through our communities, websites, apps, or publications, we inspire our audiences, bring them together, and comfort, uplift, entertain, and guide them. Visit us at guideposts.org to learn more.

We would love to hear from you. Write us at Guideposts, P.O. Box 5815, Harlan, Iowa 51593 or call us at (800) 932-2145. Did you love *Strengthened by His Touch?* Leave a review for this product on guideposts.org/shop. Your feedback helps others in our community find relevant products.

Find inspiration, find faith, find Guideposts.

Shop our best sellers and favorites at
guideposts.org/shop